Dyslexic AND UN-Stoppable

D1557118

Dyslexic
AND
UN-Stoppable

*How Dyslexia Helps Us
Create the Life
of Our Dreams and
How You Can Do It Too*

Lucie M. Curtiss, R.N.
Douglas C. Curtiss, M.D., FAAP

NEW YORK

Dyslexic AND UN-Stoppable
How Dyslexia Helps Us Create the Life of Our Dreams and How You Can Do It Too

Published in New York, New York, by Morgan James Publishing. Morgan James and The Entrepreneurial Publisher are trademarks of Morgan James, LLC. www.MorganJamesPublishing.com

The Morgan James Speakers Group can bring authors to your live event. For more information or to book an event visit The Morgan James Speakers Group at www.TheMorganJamesSpeakersGroup.com.

This is a work of nonfiction. All materials in this book are either the author's original ideas or the author's adaptation of third party ideas. As such, they represent the author's interpretations and may not necessarily represent the opinions of the persons from whom they originated.

To take advantage of all of the extras, including supplemental videos, visit:
www.DyslexicAndUnStoppable.com
Click on: Book Extras
Enter the password: Unstoppable

A free eBook edition is available with the purchase of this print book.

ISBN 978-1-63047-319-8 paperback
ISBN 978-1-63047-320-4 eBook
ISBN 978-1-63047-321-1 hardcover
Library of Congress Control Number: 2014942822

CLEARLY PRINT YOUR NAME ABOVE IN UPPER CASE
Instructions to claim your free eBook edition:
1. Download the BitLit app for Android or iOS
2. Write your name in **UPPER CASE** on the line
3. Use the BitLit app to submit a photo
4. Download your eBook to any device

Cover Design by:
Rachel Lopez
www.r2cdesign.com

Interior Design by:
Bonnie Bushman
bonnie@caboodlegraphics.com

In an effort to support local communities, raise awareness and funds, Morgan James Publishing donates a percentage of all book sales for the life of each book to Habitat for Humanity Peninsula and Greater Williamsburg.

Get involved today, visit
www.MorganJamesBuilds.com

Habitat
for Humanity®
Peninsula and
Greater Williamsburg
Building Partner

Dedication

To all the Dyslexic kids in the world
(especially my son, Félix-Alexander, also known as FéZander):
this book is dedicated to you.
Your courage and perseverance are worthy of recognition.
I'm humbled by your determination and hard work.
You are truly Dyslexic and UN-Stoppable!

Contents

Foreword

Every now and again in life you come across individuals who somehow transform the way you view the world around you. These people show up in ways and during circumstances when you least expect it. Neither the time nor the place makes any sense and yet there they are.

I have learned to stay open to such timings and places with almost an expectation of being pleasantly surprised by who or what shows up. It has not failed me yet and especially not when it comes to having met Lucie and Doug.

The lessons they have offered throughout our years of becoming friends are too many to mention here and are probably unknown even to them. Their example of unconditional love and commitment has served me on many occasions when I forget the truth of who I am.

Never could I have imagined meeting two people so in love with life and their children, as Doug and Lucie. They truly are an example of what it means to be UNSTOPPABLE!

I am honored to have them in my circle of friends and have thoroughly enjoyed their graceful understanding of a largely unknown topic such as Dyslexia. I could not have imagined that Lucie has the blessing of this particular peculiarity in her life. What a gift for the rest of us.

To FéZander and Chloé, may you be blessed in all you do and remember to offer your heart to all those you come in contact with. That truly is your greatest gift of all.

My love to you.

Martin Hahn
Lead Facilitator at Setting Hearts Free
www.settingheartsfree.com

Why I Wrote This Book

My goal in writing this book is to empower you the Dyslexic kids with tools and strategies to create the lives of your dreams and to become UN-Stoppable, to help you realize that you can achieve anything you put your minds to and to help you see that Dyslexia is a gift, a gift of creativity!

Another goal of mine is to fill your Dyslexic hearts with so much hope that all you see is possibilities in your life. You've been given an exceptional gift. It's your chance to make this world a better place. So dream big and make it happen!

Showing you the positive and encouraging side of being Dyslexic is my desire. Too many articles, books, and informational pieces focus on the so-called discouraging side of being Dyslexic. There are always two sides to a story and I want to show you the fantastic side of this story. I'm here to inspire you with actual facts, exciting possibilities, and new discoveries that make us, the Dyslexics, so valuable in this society.

That's right. You read that correctly! Dyslexics are in demand and sought out by many innovative companies. These companies are looking for the next original and brilliant idea and need visionaries who can see the world in 3-D. And, guess what, my friends? We are those brilliant people! This is one of our niches, just one example of our many talents and it's only the beginning. We are finally being recognized for our incredible thinking abilities, and we are now becoming a wonderful asset to our ever-changing and evolving society. How cool is that?

You may have been frustrated by books, with dated and useless information that discouraged you, pointing to the supposed limitations of Dyslexia, but this book is completely different. It is about hope and new beginnings with up-to-date information and real-life ideas and strategies that actually work.

This book is also about a mother and her son's journey through the world of Dyslexia. A mother and her son's quest to succeed beyond expectations in a world where Dyslexia is considered a learning disability.

It shows the experience of a mom who had Dyslexia growing up (but wasn't aware of it) in a time when Dyslexia was misunderstood and her son who is now growing up with it and knows that he's Dyslexic and was helped by age six. The difference between the two is amazing. A little help goes a very long way. And, this book shows how times have finally changed for the better for Dyslexics.

This book was written by a Dyslexic and a "right-brain thinker" (right-brain thinker's meaning will be explained in greater detail below). This book is purposely very visual and easy to read. I use simple words, concrete examples, and lots of pictures so that Dyslexics can easily understand.

Included with this book are videos posted on our website: **www.DyslexicAndUnstoppable.com** to help the Dyslexics understand and apply the tools and strategies described in this book.

I want to light a fire under every single struggling Dyslexic. I want to inspire you and help you succeed in your life. I want to give you hope. Did you know that about one out of five kids may have a learning disability? As long as we have hope, we can achieve any goal we desire. I do it all the time. When I strongly desire something, I do all I can to get it, and I usually do! I even wrote this book!

How to Best Read and Utilize This Book
for Optimal Results for the Dyslexic Reader

The first part of each chapter is written a little more from the *left-brain thinker's* perspective because I wanted to tell you my story and give you real examples. So I had to write some paragraphs, but I always kept the *right-brain thinkers* and Dyslexics in mind and kept the chapters as easy to understand as possible.

Difference Between Right-Brain and Left-Brain Thinkers

Below are a few examples of the characteristics of left-brain thinkers:

- Logical
- Objective
- Analytical
- Data oriented
- Sequential

My husband is a true left-brain thinker.

The second part of each chapter is written as "Summaries for the Right-Brain Thinkers and Dyslexics." As Dyslexics, we want the explanations and instructions short and sweet and to the point as soon as possible, in the least amount of words necessary.

Below are some of the characteristics of right-brain thinkers:

- Subjective
- Intuitive
- Creative
- Holistic
- Visual

The MOST IMPORTANT part of this book is called **"Tools and Strategies,"** and it was designed to integrate with our website, **www.DyslexicAndUnStoppable.com**, with videos specifically designed to help Dyslexics.

How could I write yet another great book packed with useful information for Dyslexics when reading is a major obstacle for them? It simply is counterproductive. I often find myself in this situation. I'm researching a topic and find a great book on the subject, but I come to find out the book is so dense with information and so exhausting to read that I simply give up and put the book away. My book is completely different because I'm Dyslexic, and I live with this reality every day. I have the same frustrations and struggles and understand what Dyslexics need to succeed.

Even in the developmental stages of writing this book, I knew that my goal was to get my message across by reaching out to the Dyslexics and helping them succeed. One morning as I was driving my kids to school, this great idea came to me: include video instructions with my book. By structuring this book completely differently than other books, this would help Dyslexics, who are known to have difficulties with reading, to understand my book by integrating videos as an accompaniment. By including videos, now all Dyslexics can follow and understand the chapter "Tools and Strategies" because they can watch the videos. They learn by watching in addition to reading. They can watch the videos over and over again on our website until they master the techniques and make them habits. Brilliant!

And another important point is that throughout my book, I intentionally only used the masculine, as using both he/she or him/her makes it very dense and tiring to read, and that would defeat the purpose of this book.

"Introduction" in Summary for the Right-Brain Thinker and Dyslexic

Go to our website www.DyslexicAndUnstoppable.com and click on the video "Introduction in Summary" (for details on how to use this book).

- Dyslexia is a gift of creativity. So be UN-Stoppable!
- Dyslexics are indispensable and sought after in this new innovative world.
- With great strategies and tools, there's hope and bright futures for Dyslexics.
- Always focus on the positive.
- Dyslexics are innovative, visionaries, fantastic problem-solvers, hard workers, determined, etc.
- The tools and strategies described in this book are used daily by a mom who has Dyslexia, whose son is Dyslexic, and whose husband (son's dad), just happens to be a pediatrician. Now, that's what I call true and tested information. (How cool is that?)
- We made videos especially for the Dyslexics.

- See the chapter "Tools and Strategies" and our website for more details!

The Word *Dyslexia*

I think the first concept we need to address in this book is the meaning of the word *Dyslexia*. Even today, there's such a stigma attached to the word *Dyslexia*. So let's take it one step at a time and start by explaining the origin/root of this word.

The word *Dyslexia* originated in the late nineteenth century.

Dys = difficult

Lexia = to read

In its simplest form, the word Dyslexia means:

difficulty with reading.

On a side note: My maiden name is Bérubé, and anyone who knows our family (the BERUBEs) knows that we love definitions and dictionaries. And, yes, even as a Dyslexic, I like them also. Two of my uncles even wrote a dictionary of acronyms! So as you can see, the use of definitions and dictionaries had to be part of this book. It is simply part of who I AM.

Now let's go back to the definition of the word *Dyslexia*.

The best explanation/definition I found was in a YouTube.com video by Kennedy/Marshall Company.

"**Dyslexia is an unexpected difficulty in reading in comparison to their intelligence, level of education or professional status.** Difficulty learning to read and the inability to read quickly, difficulty in spelling, difficulty with handwriting" (paraphrased from Dr. Sally Shaywitz, codirector, Yale Center for Dyslexia & Creativity in a video produced by the Kennedy/Marshall company).

Some people think that Dyslexia means "un-smart" and have the wrong perception about people who are Dyslexics. I'm going to say this as simply as I can so that everyone can understand. We are of normal and, in many cases, above normal intelligence, even brilliant, my friends! We are just different in the way we decode words. We learn to read differently than regular people do, but we still can learn.

I noticed that while some people are keeping track of how many pages and books I've read on the *New York Times* bestseller list, I've been busy building successful companies and making a name for myself. So I think I'm doing pretty well, right? Buy me the books as audiobooks, and I'll listen to them in my car. Until then, I'm quite happy being an **entrepreneur**! I bet you've experienced the same thing too.

Learning to read is a developed capability, a kind of process that we go through as children. For some kids it comes naturally; for others, it comes with labor and difficulty. We all can learn to read, just to different degrees. Some kids are obviously better at it than others. Reading is a learned skill as opposed to an innate ability. We learn to decode the words as we learn to read. But again, remember that words are all codes that were made up at one point to signify something we wanted to say or express. We learn to read like we learn to ride a bike. Seriously, think about it. Were you born knowing how to ride a bike, or did you learn to ride a bike? It's the same for reading. We learn by having the right tools, the right teacher, and the right strategies. Some kids become professional bikers, and others bike around the yard for the rest of their lives. And, it's all okay, as we are all different!

As Dyslexics, we have difficulty making the words on the paper and the meaning behind them stick together. When we are able to get a picture in our minds of what the word on the paper means, we can then piece the puzzle together. As soon as we visualize the meaning and associate a picture with the word, we get it. Once the connection between the two (the word and the picture) is made, we understand what the word means, and we can read it.

Sometimes people act as if Dyslexia is a communicable disease, as if they are going to catch it by talking to us. Having Dyslexia does mean we learn differently than some of you, and so what? What's the big deal? We were never supposed to all be identical. We were created to be different and unique. Each one of us has a gift inside to share with the world. How boring would the world be if we were all the same? Ever think about that? We would be robots. My desires and aspirations are too big to live the life of a robot.

Sometimes, when I say I'm Dyslexic or my son is Dyslexic, I get this look of "OMG, it's terrible. You poor thing!" Some people get very uncomfortable and immediately try to change the subject. Other times, I get responses like "That makes sense!" or "That's why your son is so smart and creative." This is so crazy! One person thinks we are slow; the other thinks we are brilliant! After many years of taking self-development courses, I now understand why people react the way they do. At that moment, that's all they know. That's their reality, and fear gets in the way. So I'm going to say it one more time, loud and clear: We Dyslexics are smart. My son even has the IQ test results just in case some of them still need more proof or convincing. We are okay with being Dyslexics. We are proud to be these creative, entrepreneurial, and brilliant right-brain thinkers!

I am one who speaks her truth, and the same goes for talking about being Dyslexic. I've always been known to put myself out there and talk about my reality. I know many people who prefer to act as if nothing were ever wrong, hard, different, or difficult. Some people go to great lengths to protect their little secrets. What you see is truly what you get with me. I'm who I am, and I like living my life that way. Just me, when I'm happy, I'm very happy. Like many Dyslexics, when I'm sad, I feel the sadness. I'm genuine and authentic, and I know people appreciate that about me as they know what to expect with me and can trust that I'm being sincere.

I noticed that I attract many people who come to me for advice, as they trust my judgment, and others who come to me just to be heard when they are having a bad day. Sometimes people need to speak about their problems without being comforted with silly sayings or interrupted with a personal anecdote to relieve the pressure of the moment. I can feel it when someone needs that kind of help, and I think that's part of being Dyslexic, as I see my son's empathy towards his sister, friends, and animals every day. He's very aware and caring. One of my friends describes my son best: "FéZander is like an old soul." I believe that it's probably related to the fact that as Dyslexics, we are so in tune with our surrounding environment. We are very visual and pay much attention to details and people's expressions. So I think that makes our senses more developed in this area. We are very good at 3-D analogies and usually have a great understanding of complex situations. We also love to solve problems and enjoy new challenges.

Dyslexia is associated with being creative and innovative! It's a gift, not a curse.

Dyslexics are:

- Perseverant
- Determined
- Creative
- Compassionate
- Empathetic
- Willing to do what's hard
- Entrepreneurial
- Visionaries

What do the following famous people have in common?

- Albert Einstein (famous physicist, $E = mc^2$)
- Steven Spielberg (director, producer)
- Richard Branson (entrepreneur, Virgin Airlines, etc.)
- Charles Schwab (Schwab Corporation)
- Pablo Picasso (artist)
- Henry Winkler (actor, director)
- Agatha Christie (world's bestselling author)
- Alexander Graham Bell (inventor of the telephone)
- George Burns (actor)
- Woodrow Wilson (former president)
- Leonardo Da Vinci (inventor, Renaissance man)
- Magic Johnson (NBA basketball player)
- Thomas Edison (inventor of the lightbulb)
- Walt Disney (Walt Disney World)
- Orlando Bloom (actor)
- John F. Kennedy (former president)
- Mozart (composer)
- Beethoven (composer)

These people have all made a tremendous impact on the world, and yes, you guessed it! They are or were all Dyslexic!

"The Word *Dyslexia*" in Summary for the Right-Brain Thinker and Dyslexic

- The word *Dyslexia*: Dys = difficulty Lexia = to read
- Simplest meaning of the word Dyslexia is: "difficulty with reading."

- Dyslexics are of normal to above normal intelligence. We are smart!
- As human beings, we learn to read as we learn to ride a bike. Dyslexics just learn to read differently than others. (Everyone needs the right tools and the right strategies to learn to read.)
- Reading is a learned skill as opposed to an innate ability.
- Dyslexics are: creative, perseverant, determined, compassionate, etc.

PART 1

The Author's Journey
with Dyslexia (1970s–Today)

CHAPTER 1

About the Author: My Story

A s you all know, we all live our lives according to our "story." The story we believe to be absolutely true without a shadow of a doubt. The story we repeat to ourselves and to others we interact with daily. The story that propels us to take action or the story that stops us dead in our tracks. You know what I mean? That little voice in our head that dictates our journey through life until the day we realize we have had enough of this story. So we decide to change it and live a different life. We can all change that story and be who we want to be, not who we think we should BE.

The following chapter recalls my story growing up, along with excerpts

Lucie at five years of age
(on vacation in the Yukon)

of my journey with Dyslexia (from childhood to the end of my college years).

This chapter shows you how I coped with Dyslexia. (**Keep in mind, I was not aware I was Dyslexic, as I only figured it out around the age of twenty-five.)

Between One and Three Years Old

One of the earliest significant indicators of Dyslexia in my life appeared between the ages of one and three years old. My parents noticed that I wasn't expressing myself verbally. Most of the time, I was quite happy just pointing to objects instead of using words to convey my needs. My vocabulary consisted of very few words and was mostly limited to gestures. And my parents were somewhat concerned at that point. Then, all of a sudden around the age of three, I leapt from speaking just a few words to full sentences without any meaningful explanation or remediation.

On a side note, I do feel compelled to mention that my Dyslexia was not "missed" because of a lack of education or a lack of involvement on my parents' part. Like most parents of Dyslexic kids, my parents wanted the best for me. My father is a brilliant doctor who was always a top student throughout his entire schooling (from elementary school to the end of medical school). And my mother is a nurse and a gifted piano player. It's just that in those days, Dyslexia was even more misunderstood than today, and parents and teachers were not as aware of it as we are now. By the way, we are talking about thirty to forty years ago, and our understanding of Dyslexia has changed and evolved drastically since those days. Remember, I'm not blaming anyone in this book. This is a book about hope and the progress we've made in the remediation of Dyslexia. In this chapter, I'm simply illustrating the difference between Dyslexia then and now, and showing you my coping mechanisms. Everyone (my parents, my teachers, my friends, my family, etc.) did the best they could at the moment, and that's all that matters.

In Elementary School

I remember when I was a little girl, I LOVED school. I was usually found sitting upright in the front row eager to learn. I would come home after school and do my homework right away, all by myself, and I never needed any help. I remember overhearing my mother talking to friends and family and saying to them how smart I was and that she didn't worry about me as I was responsible with my homework and did great in school.

Lucie in third grade

Today, looking back at my school years and old report cards with a different perspective, I now see that by third grade, signs of Dyslexia were showing up in my academic life. But in those days, we weren't fully connecting the dots. It's like putting all the evidence together after the crime has been committed. It's hard to piece it all together when it's happening. In hindsight, you can see the whole picture.

Nowadays, we know that third grade is often when Dyslexia is first recognized, since that's when kids start to read to learn new concepts and not read just to be able to sound out the words. By third grade, we need to comprehend and interpret what we are reading. Before third grade, learning to read is the main goal. By third grade, however, it is assumed that children know how to read and can use reading to explore new subjects. This is why Dyslexia becomes evident at this age.

On my third grade report card, my grades were all higher than 90 percent in every subject during all three semesters. And yet, stapled to this report card, I found a note stating that even though I had met the minimum third-grade reading objectives, my progress was unsatisfactory and that I needed to continue my oral reading every day during the summer vacation.

In another part of the report card, there was a section called "The student progresses well in reading." And each semester the teacher had to check yes or no.

First semester: The teacher checked yes.

Second semester: The teacher checked yes.

Last semester: NO check (left blank)

**Interesting, right? It all seems a little contradictory to me.

By fourth grade, subtle and understated but important changes started to take place. I remember my grades dropped one semester. At the parent-teacher meeting, my parents' divorce was an easy explanation for the fact that my grades were lower that semester. And the next semester my grades improved. Obviously, let's be honest. Nothing is black and white, so both circumstances (my parents' divorce and my Dyslexia) probably contributed to my grades fluctuating that year. But what needs to be noted here is that in most subjects my grades remained about the same, and math was the subject in question where I was having difficulties. My teacher actually wrote on my report card: "Lucie neglected her schoolwork and it shows. She could put more effort in math." Today, I know better, as I see this as a red flag. As a kid, I LOVED going to school, so why would I neglect only my math schoolwork? Also, my grades remained the same in all other subjects except math. Wouldn't I neglect other subjects along with math? Today, I have learned that this is a sign of Dyslexia. When a student is doing really well in some subjects and struggling in others, we now know more investigation needs to be done to pinpoint the cause of these inconsistencies.

**Again, interesting, right? At this point, are you seeing any similarities with your child's journey with Dyslexia?

In Middle School

I remember in seventh grade my assignment was to read an entire book from a series called *Oui-Oui*. (In Canada, I went to school in French, and these were books we used to read.) The next day we had to come to the front of the class and explain what the story was about. Boy, that book seemed so BIG and THICK. I was discouraged just looking at it. I never did read the whole book and remember standing in front of the class and going on and on about the "story" I had read. The story I mostly made up, that is. I had a great imagination, and that saved me more times than I can count. And I was often the teacher's pet. So that always helped, as they thought so highly of me as a student.

Lucie after winning a bronze medal at the Canada Winter Games (I know, I know! Please refrain from commenting on the hairdo. I'm just proving a point. We can do anything we put our minds to!)

This, by the way, is a common theme in Dyslexia. Often the kids are clever enough to "hide" their Dyslexia by figuring out their schoolwork without actually having to read it. Looking back at your child's schooling, have you noticed any similarities?

That same year we were given some type of IQ test, and my results were, of course, OUTSTANDING! So again, that solidified the idea that nothing significant was going on with me.

Out of curiosity, as I'm writing this book, I went searching online and found this famous book collection called *Oui-Oui*. And as you probably figured out by now, these books are of normal size and thickness and are much different than I remember them to be as a kid. They are age-appropriate kids' books with simple language and wording.

At the age of ten, some friends and I decided to try out the martial art called judo. From the first day, I was hooked! I loved it and was very good in competitions. For four years, I remained at the top of my category, and I also won a bronze medal at the Canada Winter Games. For all those years, I was surrounded by people who believed in me (my dad, my coach, my friends, my family, etc.).

It was a really fabulous time in my life and yet another great blessing for my self-esteem and confidence. This experience with judo and with mentors and coaches who believed in me set me off on a path of success. And today in my forties, I still do martial arts, as it keeps me active, healthy, and grounded. As a matter of fact, I practice tae kwon do with my hubby and my two kids. Imagine how great an experience it is to practice martial arts as a kid with your parents. The four of us worked together for three years and received our black belts on the same day! It is a time our family will always remember!

Finding Your Child's Strengths

 What does your child love to do? Judo was life-changing for me. Can you find something to give your child the confidence to become UN-Stoppable?

Throughout middle school, my grades fluctuated, but there was always a justifying reason, such as moving from one city to the next, moving from living with one parent to the other, changing schools in the middle of the year, judo competitions, travels, etc. There always seemed to be good excuses around the corner, and the explanations made sense at the moment.

In High School

I **NEVER** volunteered to read aloud in class and became very worried when asked to present in front of the class. My tactic was to use as many visual aids as I possibly could to accompany my presentations (pictures, drawings, slides on the projector). My biggest strengths were to be as cute and as funny as I possibly could be so that my friends wouldn't pay attention to what I was actually saying while I was doing my talk. Distraction was my method of choice to get me through those presentations, and I have to say, it usually worked out just fine. I don't remember any incident that crushed my teenage ego.

Another great clue to Dyslexia—does your child overuse "distractions" when he has to present in school? This could be a sign that he is trying to compensate for his Dyslexia.

During my last year of school, I met with the guidance counselor to help me decide my next step as I was heading to college. I can't remember how this meeting came about, but basically, it was just kind of generic. I filled out a computer questionnaire about my interests in life, and later on we sat down together and discussed the results.

All I recall him saying to me was something to the effect that I had just experienced a great loss, so it would be in my best interest to take it easy the first year of college. He suggested I take general classes with no specific major and see how it goes. This recommendation came about because the previous year I had just experienced a tragic death in my life, and I was still struggling with that loss.

I think that once again an event in my life had masked my symptoms of Dyslexia, as empathy got in the way of digging deeper into the root causes of my academic challenges. The death of my friend was an easy explanation for my struggle in school, but it didn't account for the difficulties I had experienced the previous years. So once again I remained one of those students "lost in translation." During my first year in college, I ended up in different classes than my friends and on a path that I resented (more on college coming up).

In retrospect, I wish counselors would have asked me about my hopes, my dreams, my aspirations, and what path I wanted to be on in my life. I wish they had noticed that the questionnaire results didn't match my potential and my ambitions. I wish they had gone beyond the obvious and seen that there was more to me than a few computer data analysis points. And finally, I wish they had figured out that based on my results, more investigation needed to be done. But then again, this brings up an important aspect related to the awareness of Dyslexia in those days. During that time, my school didn't know how to deal with Dyslexia and didn't offer any services anyway. Therefore, I honestly believe that I was more successful and better off left unlabeled than the alternative. I was **unknowingly** used to coping with Dyslexia by myself. And most importantly, I didn't end up mislabeled, ridiculed, and embarrassed in front of my peers because of a lack of understanding Dyslexia by the school system.

Luckily, things are better now. There is more awareness of Dyslexia. And now, with this book and our website, you have the tools and strategies to help your child overcome Dyslexia.

I personally know others who weren't so **lucky**! One in particular comes to mind because the school didn't recognize his struggles and just assumed he was being "lazy" and "uncooperative." This beautiful and truly brilliant boy's school years were extremely unbearable for him and for his parents. Thankfully, this student persevered and was able to find himself in his twenties and became the best student in his class (even the best of his college) in a programming course. Now he's living his greatest potential, and he's helping others with his gift. His determination and his mom's love were always present, and that made him UN-Stoppable!

It's a funny thing to say, but I'm actually truly grateful for slipping through the cracks and being left unlabeled. Finding out years later (after school and college were over) was a blessing in my view, as the school system was not prepared and able to help me in a positive and empowering way and could have just crushed my self-esteem. Who knows where I would have ended up? Not sure I want to know either! **Thankfully,** today that's a different story, as years of research and advancements are now coming into play. Dyslexics are blessed with great tools and information that can help them succeed in their lives, not necessarily in the traditional school system *per se*, but with a few technical skills and patience today, you can find a wealth of information. The web is now a world of knowledge and tools to help you or your child with Dyslexia. You can find everything you need from remedial schools in your area to daily exercises to do at home. The Internet is just a fantastic and crucial instrument for researching Dyslexia. It brings so much hope for so many people. I'm most definitely one of those grateful people who utilize the web to my advantage (for me and my family).

Most importantly, my hope is that this book triggers a desire in counselors to look more deeply than the obvious to make sure other patterns are not being missed. Again, I'm NOT blaming anyone. My goal is to bring awareness to the world of Dyslexia and to show the readers what it looks like from my perspective as a Dyslexic.

It's **never** too late to receive help for Dyslexia. Obviously, detecting it earlier is optimal, but getting some help at any time is better than none. I spent countless hours in the waiting room during my son's reading lessons at the private tutoring school for Dyslexics. And in that waiting room were tons of books and newsletters related to Dyslexia. I read all I could, and I learned a lot during those four years. Those references and books were a blessing put right into my hands, and it was all free and accessible. I often read about adults getting more and more help with Dyslexia. And I even found out that our current state governor was Dyslexic. Now, that's a tangible story of hope!

Report Card Comments: A Telling Story

At this point in my chapter, I want to take the time to share with you some comments made by my teachers on several of my report cards. Although certain of these comments are personally difficult to write down for the world to see, I feel compelled to show my friends, the Dyslexic kids of today, a true and accurate view of my past so they can be inspired with **actual** facts and see that **we can all succeed**!

Comments are from one extreme to another.

On the more unpleasant side, I received comments like:

- "Lucie is <u>very attentive</u> in class BUT <u>could do better in French and math</u>."
- "Lucie <u>needs to improve her handwriting</u>" (noted numerous times).
- Progress in Reading:
- Sometimes, yes
- Sometimes, no
- Sometimes, the same as last semester (I think this means NO.)
- "Lucie, <u>you can do better</u> in French and math."

- "Lucie has <u>neglected</u> her schoolwork, and <u>it shows</u>. <u>Hope she works harder</u> until June, as <u>she can do better</u>."
- "Lucie worked pretty well, <u>BUT she could make more effort in math</u>."
- "The student has <u>attained the minimum required</u> objectives in reading for third grade." (Yikes!)

On the more positive side, I received comments like:

- "Lucie does excellent work. Congrats on your great results. Continue!"
- "Lucie gave a magnificent work performance. Congrats on these great results. All along this year, you have been a remarkable student. I will keep fond memories of you."
- "Bravo, Lucie, for your progress!"
- "Lucie works well, applies herself in her work, and utilizes her time well. It's a pleasure to have you as my student."
- "Great job, Lucie. Keep it up!"
- "Lucie made progress in math and French. She is interested and takes an active part in class. Continue your great work in reading at home during the summer."
- "Excellent, Lucie!"
- "Lucie made progress in reading. Bravo!"

I received all A's (highest grade possible) across the board in all the categories below:

- **A in effort** (meaning "significant effort")
- **A for frequency** (meaning "performed consistently")
- Concentration
- Independence and work ethics

- Homework assignments
- Following directions
- Responsible
- Polite, courteous
- Respect of property and others
- Posture
- Appearance
- Well rested
- Gets along with others

When I look at all these comments I think: *Are you kidding me? How can that be? I don't understand this logic.*

These comments are contradicting each other, sometimes in the same sentence. Am I an excellent student or an unfocused student? Which is it?

Now, in retrospect, it's easy to see the big picture. The answer is quite simple because I'm on both sides of this spectrum. I am brilliant, and I also need help sometimes. I'm BOTH! That's it! This is an explanation that makes sense, and I can live with that. The most important lesson I learned looking back through my report cards is that teachers need to look at both sides of a student's progress. They need to see the student as a whole, not in fragmented parts. This part works well, but this part doesn't. If the two parts are put together and do not match up, something is wrong and needs more attention and clarification before making a final assessment. If teachers don't acknowledge both sides, they might mislabel us and lose us in the process. For example, how can I be a model student who pays attention in class and participates actively and be slacking in math all at the same time? This is a BIG red flag in my book. These are completely disconnected comments and observations, and they NEED to ring a bell, immediately!

Looking at your child's report cards, are there comments that seem to contradict each other? They could be a sign that you need to investigate further so that your child's Dyslexia is discovered early.

I have another funny personal story that demonstrates clearly this disconnection between my grades and my assumed lack of effort. In my last year in school, I received a Larousse dictionary in honor of obtaining the highest score in my French class. First of all, since elementary school, I was told I needed to spend more time studying my French lessons, and yet I ended up with the highest score in the class in my last year. Secondly, nowhere in those years did I increase my studies and practice time (you can ask my family and my friends—they know!).

I rarely studied, and I still managed to receive an honor. That's a very interesting combination in my book. The reason I remember this story so vividly is because my teacher was extremely annoyed with me because he had told me in advance that I was getting this award, but I chose to not show up at the ceremony. He had to give me the dictionary during our next class and said something to me like: "Since you didn't bother showing up for your award, I don't feel you should get this dictionary." So I received my award on a very sour note, as you can see. Looking back, I wonder if I didn't show up because deep down I felt I didn't deserve this award, since I had not worked hard for this recognition. Now I think, Wow! Imagine if I had just put in a little effort? Where would I have ended up—president of the stock exchange? I guess running a successful company comes close, right?

I kept that dictionary for many years afterwards, but eventually I donated it to the local library, as every time I would see it or research a word in it, I felt this weird negative energy associated with this entire event. I had no desire to relive this moment over and over for the rest on my life. I needed to move on from this story, so I did and got rid of it. Today, my new dictionary sits on my shelf in my office and brings joy to my life, as this one was a birthday present from my dad. Ahh . . . that's much better!

Lastly, I have a little quiz for you on the subject of teachers' comments on report cards. Which teachers do you think I remember the most? Which ones do I have the best memories of? Which ones still have a special place in my heart today?

The NICE ones who encouraged ME and BELIEVED in me! I was truly one of the **lucky** students. I mostly remembered and focused on the positive comments in my life and bypassed the others, but some students are not always so fortunate to be as stubborn and determined as I AM and may have gotten discouraged by negative feedback. For me, it just makes me persevere MORE, gives me fuel, and drives me forward. I simply refuse to give UP!

This same drive makes me want to give back to you, my fellow Dyslexics. Come to our website, www. DyslexicAndUnstoppable.com, and join our Fan Page on Facebook to connect with likeminded and UN-Stoppable people!

College and Beyond

In college, I had no idea where to put my energies. I felt lost and confused, and it showed. I changed majors, not once or twice, but seven times! I was all over the place and unfocused. I still loved science, biology, and psychology. I wanted to be a veterinarian, but I could not commit to studying and didn't know why. I even remember getting a birthday card from a friend that reminded me to study. I kind of knew I should study more, but I couldn't figure out why I didn't commit seriously to it until later on in my life. I would be so excited to listen in class, and I understood everything the teacher was explaining until he would ask us to go and buy our textbooks. OMG, they were so HUGE (and no, not the *Oui-Oui* books' size either!). I would disconnect right then and there. For years, that was the pattern for me over and over again.

I remember my biology teacher wanting to meet with me after I received a B on my test, and boy, was I scared. I couldn't imagine what he wanted to talk to me about and what was so important that I had to meet with him after class. When I finally met with him, all he said to me was, "I don't understand why you did not get an A on this test; I know you knew all the answers." He even asked me to give him the answers verbally to the questions on the test right then and there, and of course, I knew them all. I could tell he was really frustrated and disappointed with me at that moment and expected so much more from me. Even though that situation didn't change my circumstances, it had a positive impact on me. This well-liked and respected teacher saw that I was smart and wanted me to succeed. It gave me hope, and hope opens doors! Merci, Monsieur Gagné! (Thanks!) Now that's a great teacher. Teachers like that are the ones who can change a student's path in life. So, teachers, always remember that your words are very powerful and use them wisely as you might empower someone to become UN-Stoppable! Wouldn't that make your day as a teacher?

The Library

I recall this place called the "library." It was often located in the middle of the campus, and most of my friends would be in there studying. As for me, the only time I would be found in the library was when I was looking for my friends and making plans to go out that night. The library was considered a dark and dingy place in my world.

Incidentally, at this point in my life, I was so unfocused in my studies that I was mostly found sitting all the way in the back of the class and usually staring at the cute guy in front of me instead of listening to the teacher. At least, I had a great view. Today I'm happily married to one of those cute nerds I admired. My smart Ivy League–trained pediatrician hubby was most definitely one of those hot, smart guys sitting in the front row! By the way, my best friend in the whole wide world still remembers me saying back in high school that I was going to marry a smart, nerdy, and fun doctor one day. And I did! **Keep your vision clear and simple, and see miracles happen.** (I use the term "nerd" in a very loving and caring way here. I love nerds. "Nerd" means very smart and witty people in my book. They are awesome, brilliant, lots of fun, and very cute!)

One subject I really looked forward to was psychology. I am fascinated with humans and why they do what they do. I love learning about human behaviors. I understood it easily, as it just made sense to me. The only problem with college psychology classes is that they sometimes can be so boring. Some psychology classes are just too much about memorizing facts, dates, and theories. Lots and lots of theories! I craved the real-life stuff. The good and juicy stuff! Even today, I spend lots of time observing people and seeing how they live their lives, react to situations, and just deal with everyday life.

I find human psychology so intriguing and interesting to watch and discuss. On a side note, my mom has this tendency to stare at people when she likes what they are wearing. Well, sometimes I do the same as I'm observing a behavior, and my hubby usually looks at me and says, "Simone!" with a big grin of his face. Yes, you guessed right. My mom's name is Simone.

After almost five years of college and changing majors (too many times), I finally ended up in nursing school by default (another long story not worth mentioning). Looking back, it was a blessing. I found it easy enough, very practical, and I enjoyed going to the hospital and learning all the cool procedures. Procedures were my favorites, as I was really good at them, and I didn't have to memorize silly information that I would eventually never need in real life as a nurse. I think it was in my blood (as I said previously, my dad is a doctor, and my mom, a nurse.) But then again, my sister freaks out at the sight of a droplet of blood, and my brother is a lawyer! Go figure!

Being a Nurse

I was a nurse for five years when I realized that nursing was part of my path in life, but it was never my passion. I was a talented nurse, and the doctors I worked with always respected and counted on me.

In that respect, it was satisfying, but on a day-to-day basis, it was not super-interesting to me. I eventually moved on and became a business owner and managed all aspects of our company. That was much more challenging and interesting. It was a place where my creative talents were useful and where I greatly succeeded. The freedom of owning and running a very successful business has been rewarding. Today, I'm grateful for nursing, as it put me on the path to find my hubby. I'll always have good memories of my nursing days, but careerwise, I've moved on to bigger and better opportunities! I guess, in a way, I needed one successful accomplishment under my belt to show me I could make it in life, and nursing was my beginning point.

Encouraging Your Child

 Has your child had a similar experience where he may not know exactly what he wants to do in life? That's okay. Encourage him to explore different interests. You never know where it will lead him.

"About the Author: My Story" in Summary
for the Right-Brain Thinker and Dyslexic

- An early sign of Dyslexia is having speech and language issues.
- Reading: Third grade is frequently when reading issues become apparent to parents and teachers.
- Ask your child to describe how it feels to read a book:
  - "What do you see when you are trying to read?"
  - "Are the words moving on the page?"
  - "Are the pages blurry?"
- Pay very close attention to comments made by teachers/counselors/coaches about your child. Look for inconsistencies or red flags.
- Examples:
  - Your child is very attentive in class but could do better in math.
  - Your child is a great listener, but his homework needs improvement.
- If you see the following words in your child's report card, do more investigation to rule out Dyslexia:
  - Lack of effort
  - Lazy
  - Inconsistent
  - Fine motor difficulties
  - Uncooperative
  - Unfocused
  - Distracted
  - Difficulty reading
  - Can't remember math facts

- ○ Laborious writing
- ○ Struggling with reading aloud
- If you see your kid is spending hours at night doing homework for a task that should take no more than fifteen to twenty minutes, or if he's struggling and has difficulty finishing his assignments, it's time to talk to the teachers.
- Check out the video on our website on "Lack of effort" for more clues and red flags.
- Parents, if you suspect your child is struggling or has Dyslexia, ask him lots of questions about how he feels, his dreams in life, his hopes, and see if it matches the patterns above. Our son FéZander, since he was three or four years old, talked about wanting to be an engineer but had difficulties with math facts. So we knew that his struggles with math facts were legitimate and he needed help to overcome this problem, as he loves math.
- Teachers, choose your words very carefully with your students, as they are very powerful. Use your words to do good in a child's life and see him become UN-Stoppable.
- Find something your child likes to do and focus on it. Along with activities we enjoy come great adventures, positive reinforcement, remarkable teachers and mentors, and a lifetime of wonderful memories.

CHAPTER 2

Ahhh, a Sigh of Relief!
Finally, a Logical Explanation!

n my mid-twenties (winter of '97), I graduated from nursing school and moved to the United States to work as a pediatric nurse in a private practice. (I'm Canadian.) In the United States, English is the main language, so it took some adjusting for a while since my first language is French, but eventually I managed.

Lucie's graduation picture from nursing school (much better hairdo!)

One of my many responsibilities as a nurse was to call prescriptions for patients to the local pharmacies. This task seemed simple enough until I was faced with multiple obstacles.

- **Obstacle #1: Language barrier:** I had a thick French accent, and the pharmacists and technicians sometimes had difficulty understanding me over the phone.

- **Obstacle #2: Patients' names:** I had to spell the names of patients, as some were quite different from what I was used to. I had no idea how to pronounce many of the names I encountered.
- **Obstacle #3: *G* and *J*, and *E* and *I*:** To add to this mix was a confusing difference between the French and English languages. In the French language *G* and *J*, and *I* and *E* are pronounced the opposite of the English language. In other words, if I encountered the name James, I had to think, "How do you say that first letter? Is it 'gee' or is it 'jay'?" How confusing is that?
- **Obstacle #4: S and C:** And on top of the obstacles above, I often say *C* when I actually mean *S* and vice versa. Throughout my life, I had noticed that sometimes I interchange *S* for *C*. For example, if I had to spell "Samuel," I would be seeing and thinking *S* in my head, but the word that would come out of my mouth would be "Camuel." On occasion, I noticed and corrected myself right away, and other times, I would be oblivious to it until someone pointed it out to me. (Some people are experts at pointing out our mistakes. They are eager and happy to correct us without giving us a second to figure it out for ourselves, right?)

Do you notice that people are quick to correct you when you speak or read? Always remember, this has little to do with you. It is more about their insecurities and their need to be right. Let it roll off your back, and STAY UN-Stoppable!

By now you can see that the act of simply calling in prescription refills was turning into a nightmare for me. At first, it was stressful. Then everyone at the office got to know me and found out about my little issue. So eventually it became an amusing joke around the office, and we ended up having fun with it. I even got a new nickname: EKG! EKG because, when I would call to set up an EKG at the hospital, the technician gave me a hard time and told me to call back when I knew the test I wanted to order. Of course, I knew exactly what I needed to order, but the person on the line didn't like the way I would pronounce EKG! I was obviously hitting a nerve with that person, and it had nothing to do with me.

Because my issue with *S* and *C* was bugging me like crazy, I decided to investigate it a little more to see where it was coming from and why I was having this difficulty. So, as I usually do when I need help, I picked up the phone and called my dad.

On the phone, I explained my situation to my dad, and I was going on and on about it like a lunatic.

I eventually took a pause to take a breath of air, and my dad finally got a chance to put a word in the conversation and said: "When you were a little girl, I think around fourth grade, I noticed that you were interchanging *S* and *C*. So I mentioned it to the teacher. All this time I thought it had been taken care of a long time ago."

"What?" I'm thinking, "You knew all along? How come we never talked about this? What's wrong with me?" And on and on it went in my head.

Eventually I calmed down, came back to earth, and started searching to find out how I had missed that. I've never heard of anyone with Dyslexia in my family history. So even today, I'm perplexed by the idea of how I ended up with it. (Hmm, maybe it will be part of my second book as a self-discovery journey I will take.)

As I thought about it some more, I realized my Dyslexia was left unlabeled partly because I had never brought any of this up in a conversation. This subject was just never mentioned, since I rarely asked for help with homework and never read books or spelled words aloud in front of people. So time passed, and this little glitch remained a mystery.

I began connecting the dots and researching to find answers to this annoying spelling problem. As I started asking more questions and digging into my past, it all became apparent to me when I put all the evidence together. "I'm Dyslexic! There's actually a name for it—Dyslexia. Yes! It all makes sense now."

"I was once lost, but now I'm found." Figuring out that I had Dyslexia opened doors for me and helped me see that I'm okay just the way I AM. And nursing helped me figure out I'm Dyslexic. Finally, I felt a HUGE sigh of relief, as I had an explanation to all my years of struggling and wondering. I finally enjoyed some peace of mind knowing it had a name—*Dyslexia*. PHEW! Now I could move on with my life, right? Not so fast . . . I was embarking on another journey. Now I needed to help someone else succeed in life—my son!

"Ahhh, a Sigh of Relief! Finally, a Logical Explanation!"
in Summary for the Right-Brain Thinker and Dyslexic

- Dyslexia can be overcome, remediated, and at the same time will always remain part of your life. Get used to being Dyslexic and accept it, and then you'll see the possibilities grow around you. It's a gift! Believe in yourself as you are perfect exactly the way YOU ARE!
- If you notice you have difficulties or you are struggling with reading, math, spelling or whatever, tell your parents as soon as possible so they can get you the help you need. Take care of yourself, as you are the

only one who really knows what's going on inside of your body.

- Have the courage to speak up for yourself. YOU ARE worth it!
- It's NEVER too late to get help for Dyslexia.
- A sign of Dyslexia is interchanging letters. (I interchange C and S.)
- Another sign of Dyslexia is reversing numbers. (I make up new phone numbers all the time!)
- Learning and speaking a second language can be tricky for a Dyslexic. And, at the same time, it is very helpful with the rewiring of the brain. So keep learning and trying! Even though it can be challenging, you'll be glad you did. Give those neurons a workout!
- I personally prefer to know that I'm Dyslexic, and my son feels the same way. It's a big relief to get an explanation and a name to associate with our glitch. You may choose to keep it to yourself, and that's perfectly ok. As long as you know what's going on with yourself, you can move on, get help, and enjoy your journey!

CHAPTER 3

Back into Learning!

For years, I've been taking self-development classes and business courses for "real life," and those kinds of trainings are fabulous. They are experiential, informative, and visual. Just my kind of learning and I can't get enough! We get to travel all around the country and learn all at the same time. We've met incredibly smart, interesting, funny, and just amazing people. Some of the teachers are very famous people known all over the world, and others are simply incredibly awesome teachers who are willing to put themselves out there and serve the world by being the best they can be! I seriously recommend it for everyone. It expands your way of thinking, brings out your creativity, and grows your database of knowledge to infinity where all you see are possibilities. This is a learning environment where everyone helps each other succeed and become the best they can be. It's simply magical to see people working together to create a better world, a place where people feel compelled to help you succeed.

You simply get addicted to learning! I even ran into friends of friends from where I grew up in a small town in New Brunswick, Canada. That was really cool! I heard their accent, and right away I knew they were from my part of the world. (Actually, my hubby heard them first! So funny!)

Today, now in my forties, I'm back to sitting the closest I can to the stage or the teacher (second row, in the middle, in the VIP section). You can always find me there! It even stirs up some people at the classes, as they get very upset with me for always being early and getting the seat I want. We are talking about five hundred to eight hundred people in a class here. If I can't get my spot, somehow someone is saving it for me. It's quite amusing to see. It used to bother me when people would come to me and say things like, "You can't always sit there. We want to sit there too." But I finally realized that the people who complained were usually the ones showing up late and trying to blame me for them not having the front seats (I was their punching bag), and the go-getters and committed ones would be the ones saving my seat. Interesting, right? Listen, there's plenty of seats reserved in the VIP section; two seats won't make a difference. If you want that seat, get in line, and stay in line.

Well, now I know better. Successful people want to help others, and unsuccessful people want to blame others for not being successful. I learned a great lesson. Associate with rich and successful people and you will attract wealth and success. But there's a catch here. I'm talking about rich and successful people with **integrity**. A jerk is a jerk whether he's rich or poor. I'm talking about the ones who are willing to put themselves out there and show their flaws as well as their successes and want others to succeed also.

I'm often the first one waiting at the door or, for sure, one of the first ones at the door. That's how I live my life. I show up and show up early, always! Everyone who knows me knows that if I'm late, something's wrong! Sorry. I get distracted and talk about ten things at once. Ask my hubby. He knows, but he understands me, and that's all that matters.

 You may have noticed people complaining about your successes. When they see you do something outstanding, they try to bring you down. Get used to it. It is going to happen. As a Dyslexic, it's your nature to think of different and amazing new things. Dyslexics are the ones who change the world. If someone complains, invite him to join you. If he chooses differently, realize that it has nothing to do with you. Let it go, and continue to do amazing things in your life!

I want to learn and grow. I want to be in positive energy and have a wonderful experience. I'm taking the time to be there, and I want to enjoy every moment. I want to continue learning and growing just as I did when I was little girl. That willingness to learn is stronger now that I know I'm okay and I don't have to pass the tests. I'm here to grow and have fun, all the while learning. Learning is fun, learning is growing, and learning is enjoying being alive!

"Back into Learning!" in Summary for the Right-Brain Thinker and Dyslexic

- ALWAYS keep learning!
- Expand your horizon! There's a beautiful world and many amazing people out there still to be discovered.
- Listen to others with an open mind and open heart. Listen!

- Learn one new thing every day!
- Stay connected with like-minded people.
- Have FUN, SMILE, and LAUGH at least once a day! Enjoy your life!
- How do you show up in your life? Look at your patterns and habits as they apply in all aspects of your life (family, friends, career, etc.).
  - Are you on time, early, or late?
  - Do you keep your commitments to yourself and others?
  - Do you speak your truth with compassion?
  - Do you blame others for your quality of life?
  - Do you attract successful people or unsuccessful people into your life?
  - Are you always rushing, running, stressed out, overworked, underpaid, and on and on?
  - Are you **grateful** for your life, your family, your kids, the sun, the butterflies, and a beautiful rainbow, or do you complain all the time?
- Look inside to see what it all means. It's all about YOU. You choose every moment of every day. Are you making the right choices for yourself?

CHAPTER 4

Coping (Part One)

L ooking back through my school years, now that I know I'm Dyslexic, I understand why I did what I did. (See if you recognize the signs of Dyslexia now that you know more about it too.) The first thing to remember is that I had no idea I was Dyslexic until I was twenty-five years old. And the second thing to remember is, of course, I still have some of those symptoms today, as you can remediate Dyslexia, but it will always be with you. Dyslexia is just part of my DNA, like my big blue eyes. And I wouldn't change a thing. I'm happy just the way **I AM**.

Reading

- I look at a book with many words and get discouraged before I even open the first page.
- I sometimes read the same paragraph over and over and still I don't always understand or remember what I just

read. This is especially true with black and white pages and chapter books. By the way, my whole entire family (from my siblings all the way to my aunts and uncles) and my in-laws are all awesome, fantastic, excellent, and advanced readers. So believe me, **I feel the pressure,** but it doesn't ever stop me! Thank you, audiobooks! I **love** audiobooks! They are my lifesavers.

- I ABSOLUTELY, without a shadow of a doubt, dislike and have an aversion to reading aloud.

- I'm still a slow reader, but I'm improving more and more as time goes by. I try reading every day even when I don't feel like it. I read subjects I enjoy so it makes it worth the effort. As Dyslexics, we may not be the best readers, but we still need to practice, as it is part of life, and we need to be able to read even if it's not PERFECT! Perfection is not the goal. So please always continue reading. **Don't ever give up on yourself!**

Writing

- I press **really** hard on my pencil when writing. My fingers hurt after a while, and it takes me longer to write a letter by hand than by typing on the keyboard. This is a feature of dysgraphia that is part of Dyslexia. Thank you also for computers, my other lifesaver.

- As I'm writing this, I'm looking sideways at my paper instead of sitting in front of it, and I tilt my head to the side as I write. My alignment between my pencil and my eyes is not straight.

- I tilt and position my paper to the side when writing instead of keeping the paper straight in front of me.

- I find it difficult to write and take notes when someone is speaking. It sometimes feels as if it's all going too fast, and I get disoriented. Thank you for smartphones! Now I can just take a picture of the notes on the big screen! Life in the technology world is **FANTASTIC** for ME!

- I find I easily get lost and make more mistakes when people are watching me. It makes me nervous, and then I can't concentrate. I feel like I'm sitting on a big blank cloud in my head, and time is passing by as I'm trying to refocus my thoughts. So annoying, but true!

- I mix uppercase and lowercase letters when writing. When I take my time, I have great penmanship, but when I'm in a hurry, forget it. I can't even understand what I wrote, and I'm NOT a doctor, as you know!

 What habits do you have when you read and write? Are there some that serve you? How do you compensate? Do you use technology to make your life easier? Come to our Fan Page on Facebook and tell us your story.

Miscellaneous

- I dislike using the phone and especially having to take a message, as I often write down the wrong number. I can easily write 45 instead of 54, and *S* and *C* reversal shows up again for me, so Samuel can become Camuel. One more thank you for answering machines and voice mail! Yet another lifesaver for **ME**!

- Left and right. "Which left and which right? This one or that one?" That's my biggest challenge with doing tae kwon do. *Forms* are all about precision. *Forms* are an art by themselves. You have to be exactly to the left this way and exactly to the right that way. There's no room for errors. Everyone is watching as you are being judged by the MASTERS. No PRESSURE, right? Of course, there's LOTS of pressure!

Forms are definitely not my strongest point, but I manage to get through each time and come out okay. Testing is about every two months, and I've been doing tae kwon do for the past four years, so it keeps me on my toes. We need challenges to grow. It doesn't stop me one bit. Just keep trying. If you don't quit, you never fail. I worked my b— off, and now I'm a proud black belt. I told you. **You** can do anything you put your mind to. The most important lesson I learned at tae kwon do is that everyone has strengths and weaknesses, and as long as we help each other out, we can all succeed. This sport is all about sportsmanship, collaboration, and perseverance. Plus, I throw a mean punch, and I'm a powerful board breaker. So don't mess with me! (We all have our black belts in my family, and we did it all together at the same time—my hubby, the two kids, and I. So **watch out!**)

- I still have difficulty pronouncing some words. I can hear and see it correctly in my head, but it somehow comes out differently when I say it aloud.

- I hold my head a lot with my hand while thinking, writing, and just sitting. (By the way, I'm actually doing it as I'm writing these words—wild!) And my son does the same exact gesture. For me, that's always a clue that I need to refocus my son's attention because now I know that in that moment he's not using both sides of his brain to think. He's now aware of it also. So I just remind him to place his nondominant hand back on the paper or table so he can use both sides of his brain to finish his task. Now that we know how to deal with this problem, we just do it, and it's no big deal. It's so fascinating to watch and so easy to remediate.

- I literally can think of ten things at the same time and talk about two different subjects in one conversation. My imagination is very active. So it makes me great at multitasking, which women love to do. Not a trait my hubby has any desire to achieve in his lifetime. "Let's take care of one situation at a time" is his motto. But he still puts up with me, so that's all that matters. Me, I'm like, let's **GO— NOW**!

- When I was in high school (I'm dating myself here and it's okay), I would record myself on audiotapes reading my school textbooks and listen back to the tapes to see if I could retain the information better (not even knowing why I was doing that). I had heard on TV about some study in China where they would have people listening to audiotapes while sleeping, and it would help them be smarter and better at remembering facts. It sounded good at the time, but as you probably figured out, it didn't do much for me.

- Highlighters: When **highlighters** came into vogue, I remember thinking, "Those are so cool." I would highlight my notes like crazy and organize my folders with awesome dividers, but I never quite got to the actual studying of the material I so joyfully highlighted. My notes and textbooks looked great, though!

- Math facts: Today I'm still not Speedy Gonzalez at remembering math facts like multiplications (factor 9's especially).

- My mind thinks quicker than I can write my words on paper. It sometimes feels like I can't get everything on paper fast enough to keep up with my thoughts and all the ideas flowing through me.

- I speak quickly because sometimes I feel that if I don't say it fast enough, I may lose my train of thought. I'm aware of it now, so I try to catch myself and slow down when I can.

- I have a vivid imagination, and I think in pictures instead of words.

- I have a multidimensional perception. I see ideas in 3-D.

- I'm highly intuitive and insightful. I feel things more than I logically think of them. (My gut feeling, or sixth sense, guides me.)
- I have this 3-D vision of life. I can see and feel in my mind how a project will end up looking even before I start working on it. I see the BIG picture. I can visualize the entire scenario and look at it from different angles, even when I'm in the beginning phase of a new project.
- I always come up with great innovative and creative ideas to fix a situation or make something happen, but I'm not necessarily comfortable with people who are very pushy and who want an answer right away. You know those people who drill you for answers instead of having a conversation with you? They want an immediate answer to every single question they ask you, and they expect the answers to be short, fast, and quick. I call them the "drill sergeant."
- I quickly get uncomfortable in those situations, as I don't enjoy having those kinds of conversations and prefer to be given a chance to actually think for a moment of what I really want to respond. Those interactions usually leave me feeling unsatisfied with my answers and give me a feeling of being drained by just trying to keep up with the grueling questioning.

Look over your life and habits. What have you developed to help you cope? Are there compensations that work for you? Do you also have quirky habits that seem different from everyone else's? Focus on what works for you, and let go of the rest.

When I take self-development classes, one thing I truly appreciate is when a successful person talks about his journey to success. He is willing to talk about the hard times and the difficulties and how he persevered to get to where he is now—and when you can see in his eyes that he wants you to succeed also and will help you along the way. Now that's an amazing person! I always aspire to be that kind of person. Help one Dyslexic child or a parent of a Dyslexic child. Give them hope, strategies, and some good resources. That's my goal.

"Coping (Part One)" in Summary for the Right-Brain Thinker and Dyslexic

- Signs of reading difficulties I encountered:
  - Laborious reading
  - Taking lots of deep breaths while trying to read
  - Difficulty remembering or understanding what I just read
  - Getting discouraged by the size of the book
  - Disliking reading aloud
  - Slow reader, especially with complex wording and phrasing
  - I am so grateful for audiobooks! Thank you!
- Signs of writing difficulties I encountered:
  - I press really hard on my pencil when writing.
  - My fingers hurt after long periods of writing.
  - When rushed, my handwriting is often illegible.
  - Computers are my new best friends!
  - I have a misalignment between my paper, hand, and head when writing.

- o I can do only one thing at a time when I'm writing, and that's writing. Just forget about trying to listen, write, and look at the board/screen all at the same time. Now I take it one step at a time or use my phone to take a picture!
- o I easily get lost and make more mistakes when people are watching me when I'm trying to write.
- o I use a mixture of uppercase and lowercase letters when I write. I invent my own punctuation and make up many symbols as I see fit when taking notes. For example, I have drawn a stick figure to signify an individual or a person in my book for as long as I can remember. Nursing school was fantastic, as we had tons of symbols for word meanings. That was really awesome! (NPO, PRN, BID, QID, RX, and on and on). Short and sweet. Just the way I like it!
- The phone:
  - o Leave me a detailed message, and I'll call you back later.
  - o (After I've listened to the message ten times.)
  - o I'm great at making up new phone numbers: 203 becomes 302.
- Samuel becomes Camuel as I interchange *S* and *C*.
- Left and right: Still trying to figure that one out.
- Speech:
  - o I mispronounce words, as the grammar rules are "unsticky" in my head. I see and hear a word in my head clearly, but it comes out differently when I say it aloud.

- ○ I interchange words like:
    - ◊ as/has
    - ◊ want/won't
    - ◊ to/too
    - ◊ are/our
  - ○ I sometimes speak really quickly. It feels as if I need to speak fast so I don't lose my train of thought so I get to say all I want to say. I'm aware of this now, so I try to s-l-o-o-o-w down and BREATHE.
- I hold/rest my head in my hand a lot.
- I can think of ten things at the same time and talk about two different subjects in one conversation.
- Math facts: I'm no Speedy Gonzalez at remembering math facts, but I can manage. Factor 9 is still confusing, so I take my time!
- My thoughts come quicker than I can put them on paper. Now I use my voice recorder on my phone. Then I transcribe it on paper later. I can replay my notes as often as I want. It's such a great tool for ME and makes my life so much easier and less stressful!
- I have a vivid imagination, and I come up with great ideas. I see ideas in 3-D, as I have a multidimensional perception of the world. When I can visualize it, I can make it happen.
- I'm highly intuitive and insightful. My gut feeling often comes in handy.
- I'm great at seeing the big picture and creating successful projects. Other medical practices have even approached us to copy some of our promotional models. Cool, right?

- I enjoy starting new challenges and putting plans into action.
- I love being an entrepreneur and creating!

Coping (Part Two)

How I'm coping today as a business owner, manager, and entrepreneur:

Two very important words come into play.

DELEGATION and SYSTEMATIZING

Many people may think that you need to know all the answers to every challenge. What I have found as a Dyslexic and an entrepreneur is that I can always find someone who has the answer I need. I can focus on what I do best and make alliances with people who complement my strengths.

I Work from Home

I have a designated quiet working space in my home where I can think clearly, be productive, and concentrate with limited distractions. As the business manager, I'm in charge of all aspects of our company's finances, employee payroll, and marketing strategies, just to name a few. This setup is ideal, as results show by increased productivity and a more efficient work ethic. A big part of our success is in part due to the fact that I have a designated off-site space to gather important information, to assess situations, and have a quiet place to think of solutions to problems that arise. This is the only job at our company than can be done off-site, and this is actually why we are a very efficient and productive company.

The environmental distractions are removed, and the space is conducive to success, which is extremely difficult to do otherwise in a normal workplace setting. All other jobs in our practice need to be done on-site, as they are directly related to patient care or staff. For example, physicians can't diagnose ear infections by telepathy; it's just the nature of the business.

 In this fast-paced, online society, it is now easier than ever for you to craft a career like mine. Think of ways that you can use technology to make a career arrangement that works for you and offers you the space and time to think and be creative. Then you will see yourself flourish.

I'm Extremely Organized

Being organized is crucial to running a business successfully. It's essential for me to have monthly folders to keep track of bills and to-dos. I need to know and remember what's due and when (sometimes even up to a year in advance). For example, when July comes around, I take out my July folder and see what needs to be taken care of that month. My July folder holds everything that needs to be addressed for July. It can be as simple as paying a specific bill on time. My folder can hold reminder notes from a meeting from six months ago or just a quick sticky-note message to follow up on a previous situation, but it works beautifully, and it's super easy to do.

I use a calendar for my daily tasks. Every day I check my calendar and see what needs to be done. I try to put in practice what I have learned at my business courses (the most important task needs to be done first thing in the morning).

I use my phone alarm system for all kind of reminders. It's a great tool to send reminders, gather to-do lists, or just to jot down an important note or brilliant idea while on the go.

I use voice mail. I can listen to a message five hundred times to get the name and phone number right (I'm exaggerating, but you get the point). It's not helpful when the person leaving the message speaks super fast and unclearly. That's not me being Dyslexic, but rather the messenger being inconsiderate. Please, slow down!

I have an office manager on-site who's in charge of phone messages and incoming calls. Any message that needs my attention gets sent to me via e-mail, so this way the information is already written down for me. E-mail is a great tool, and I utilize it as much as I can.

I use online banking and company websites as much as possible. There's just so much we can do online nowadays. It simplified my life greatly, and I'm grateful for all those helpful tools.

"Coping (Part Two)" in Summary for the Right-Brain Thinker and Dyslexic

- Delegation and systematizing are crucial to succeed as a Dyslexic in the workplace.
- Knowing the right people who can help you is key. The goal is to surround yourself with knowledgeable people

who can help you when needed. Knowing everything about everything is overrated, exhausting, and is an impossible goal in the first place.

- Work in a quiet space, or set up quiet time for important tasks. Ask for privacy when needed for demanding tasks so you can focus better.
- Get organized, and stay organized. You'll be much happier in the long run.
- Use your smartphone as a tool for taking notes (voice messaging), keeping track of your appointments in your calendar, and setting alarms for important reminders, just to name a few.

CHAPTER 6

What Do Dyslexia and Having Kids Have in Common? Determination *and* Perseverance!

In my mid-twenties, I met the man of my dreams and we got married. We both wanted kids, so we started working on having our little family right away. The only glitch was that we were aware I had a fibroid that might cause problems. Well, saying we had a problem is putting it mildly! I got pregnant, all right, and ended up with a humongous fibroid and a molar pregnancy. And they were both growing like crazy at the same time.

FéZander and Dada catching up on sleep at the hospital

To my great fortune, I married a Yale-trained pediatrician, and we had recently relocated close to Yale Hospital, as we had just bought a private practice in the area. How much more could I ask for? It was the perfect timing with the highest quality care (I was in excellent hands!). I had three

Yale docs, and they were ALL the best of the best. In French, we say *la crème de la crème*! First, there was my ob-gyn (Dr. David Lima), who is a fabulous and caring doctor. He just took such good care of me, calling me every week and sometimes twice a week to check on me. I definitely must have given him gray hairs. To this day, I'm still the most challenging and complex case he ever had. My chart was so thick. It was amazing. Now we have EMR (electronic medical records); it's not as impressive, since you cannot actually see the size of your chart. When he removed the molar pregnancy, half of his practice was in the operating room. It was just incredible. My case was so complex that it's one to be discussed in the ob-gyn journals.

The doctor who helped remove my molar pregnancy was none other than Dr. Ernest Kohorn, THE world-renowned expert in molar pregnancies (told you I'm a lucky lady). He even invented the blood test for tracking it. And my third doctor was, Dr. Aydin Arici, a Yale reproductive endocrinologist who specialized in removing fibroids. After the surgery was done, Dr. Arici told my hubby that he had been doing myomectomies (removing fibroids) for over twenty-five years, and THIS one was the most challenging he had ever performed. Yikes!

This reminds me of a funny story. When I was pregnant, I had to be careful at the end of my pregnancies because of the high risk for bleeding due to the major surgeries I just had the year before. I was not allowed to even have one single contraction, which sounded quite good to me since it meant no painful contractions. Anyway, at the end of my pregnancy for my daughter (late August), it was a beautiful Saturday, and we wanted to go for a last sail for the summer. Only problem was, I had to be no more than thirty minutes away from Yale Hospital in case of an emergency. To show you how serious it was, I even had my ob-gyn's beeper number (not his office phone number, but his actual beeper number) in case we both had to rush to the hospital and meet there. So we decided to go sailing with my in-laws on their boat, but we could not leave the harbor. So imagine this: a beautiful sunny day and a big sailboat sailing around and around in circles on Long Island for hours next to the harbor. Wouldn't you think, "These people are crazy! What are they doing?" Nonetheless, we had fun, and my hubby got to sail one last time before the summer ended, and I was safe.

A big part of my success with all the surgeries was my attitude throughout this ordeal. I remained optimistic and positive. I chose to look at the bright side of this journey, and I was convinced that it would end up just fine. My secret was quite simple. I had faith, and I was grateful for the fabulous care I was given. Gratefulness has been my ally my whole life. It's a very powerful tool. My ob-gyn would sometimes say, "I can't believe you're still smiling with what you are going through!"

 When apparent challenges come up in your life, take a few seconds to be grateful for all of the wonderful people and things in your life. You'll feel better, and you'll be able to refocus your energy and overcome any obstacle.

I'm one of those people who doesn't care about the Joneses' or the neighbors' opinion. I enjoy my wonderful life. I travel, I have my own company, and I work to make a difference in the world. I love bringing hope to kids who are going through a difficult time by volunteering. That alone puts me instantly in a state of gratitude, and gratitude is what makes life meaningful. I encourage and support my kids to be who they are, and they amaze me more and more as they get older and become confident in their own skin.

I don't care what car, clothes, or vacation people think I should have, wear, or go to. If I like it, I do it; and if I don't like it, I just don't. Life is too short to settle. I'm willing to put myself out there, try new challenges, fail at some and be successful at others. I don't live the "comfortable" life.

I live in the moment. I want to experience life, not just go through the motions day in and day out, and that's by choice.

You too can choose a better life for yourself. Rather than point the finger at your boss, kids, mate, environment, circumstances, friends, parents, teachers, or cat, ultimately, it's all about you. You make the decisions, and no one else is responsible for your life. You don't like your life? Make a change, and see opportunities come your way.

 Look at your own life. Think of areas where you may be complaining rather than taking accountability. Choose to take responsibility, and watch possibilities for change open up for you.

Determination drives me. As I'm writing this book, I'm up at 5:00 a.m. to have quiet creative time; I'm driving two hours a day bringing my kids to school (my kids go to two different schools in two different towns); I run our successful company and still find time to fix my house, garden, landscape, go to tae kwon do, and also find time to enjoy my family. So now you see, we Dyslexics are determined and can do anything our hearts desire. It's just a commitment away. And yes, we are UN-Stoppable!

As a final note on my story, I want to talk about my biggest fear in life—stage fright! My whole life it held me back, as I was sometimes uncomfortable with my speech and articulation, but now I'm done letting that stop me. It always bugs me when people don't understand what I'm saying. Either they say, "What did you say?" and make me repeat myself over and over again, or they correct me, thinking if they do so, I'll say it better next time. It used to just shut me down and make me angry.

Now I try to put the comment on a cloud and move on. (Not the easiest thing to do but I'm getting better every day!)

At any rate, I'm letting go of this fear and facing it straight on. In late October, I'm attending a class called "Train the Trainer" with my hubby. This course is ALL about public speaking and getting over your fears. It's also about how to run seminars and talks and how to do presentations in public. I'm scared silly, but I'm doing it. What new challenge are you going to attempt today?

"What Do Dyslexia and Having Kids Have in Common? Determination *and* Perseverance!" in Summary for the Right-Brain Thinker and Dyslexic

- Success is all about ATTITUDE. Believe in it and it will come true!
- Gratefulness (as corny as it may sound) IS the key to happiness. The more you are grateful for all your blessings, the more blessings you get. (I'm not a religious person per se, so I'm not being moral with you.) I'm simply saying to give thanks for what you have and you'll get more of it! Try it, and let me know how it goes. It's been tried and tested and is guaranteed to work.
- Determination is another key to success, and Dyslexics usually are very determined and perseverant people. Unless you are Dyslexic or have a Dyslexic child, you are usually oblivious to how hard Dyslexics work on a daily basis.
- It is extremely hard work to remediate difficulties with reading, speech, math, and writing. It's intense and constant. And you have to put in long hours of practice time before results show. Determination is our middle name!

- We all have fears. So what are you going to do about it? Freeze or move forward? I choose to move forward! How about YOU?
- Being Dyslexic will never stop me from achieving my dreams. I'll go through, around, or under any obstacle and find a way to make it work, and so can YOU.

Be UN-Stoppable with ME!

PART 2

The Author's Son's Journey
with Dyslexia Today

CHAPTER 7

The Second Time Around, We Caught It Early!

I n this chapter, I will describe some of the early signs of Dyslexia in my son. The most recognizable symptoms showed up in kindergarten and first grade. Reading difficulty was the biggest clue that something was going on with our son. While there were always other excuses to explain any issues, this time we did not let them stop us. We knew to dig deeper to the actual cause of the issue.

Birth to One Year Old

The first six months, FéZander progressed as expected, with the exception of a tremendous case of

FéZander (twenty-two months old) with Dada at the beach (Halloween party)!

colic (a topic for another book). Developmentally, a couple of things stuck out:

- Very early crawler (started at five months old). Relentless climber. UN-Stoppable

FéZander was climbing everywhere all day long! No rest for Maman.

FéZander (ten months old). Yes, ten years later, we look at these pictures and think the same thing as you: "How did he get up there, and how did we not stop him?" Already, he was the epitome of UN-Stoppable!

- He climbed and climbed and climbed!

One to Three Years Old

As far as gross motor skills, FéZander continued to develop normally to advanced. However, his language seemed a little behind his peers. Just as when I was growing up, there was an easy excuse. For FéZander, we attributed it to the fact that he was learning two languages, French and English. Looking back, we now realize it was part of his Dyslexia.

Preschool

There was no big noticeable issue in preschool that would have given us a clue that he was Dyslexic. Only thing that comes to mind is the fact that a lot of people in America choose to hold their kids back, especially if they are boys and are born between July and December. We didn't see the need for that, as FéZander was obviously smart and eager to go to kindergarten. The fact that he was small for his age didn't help, as people kept thinking he was younger than he actually was. But in the end, we made the right choice for him and would redo the same today, and **that's all that matters.**

By the way, my hubby is my height, and when people would make these assumptions (boy, December birth, and smaller than his peers), he had a fantastic reply: "I would still be in seventh grade if I had been evaluated on my size." (He's also an October baby who went to kindergarten on time and obviously did great!)

Four to Five Years Old (Kindergarten)
Fine Motor Skills

FéZander had difficulty forming letters and numbers correctly, and at the same time, he had great fine motor skills (he was already building complex Legos). These two distinctions can easily be missed but are very important to recognize. Even though the two tasks seem to involve fine motor skills, writing requires a different area of the brain. It relies heavily on the ability of information to flow from one side of the brain to the other. As such, one can be very dexterous yet still have writing issues.

Writing

When he had to read and write at the same time, he needed support. The teacher wrote, "He tires easily, which may be related to his late birthday."

Here again, three things ALWAYS came up:

- Boy
- December birth
- He was a little guy

My hubby would often joke, "It's time for me to go in and meet the teacher so they can see size is not the issue. Look at me. Size never stopped me!"

Reading

First Semester

The teacher's note: "He enjoys listening to stories and participating in discussions about books." At the time, he was mostly listening to the stories read in class and was not yet required to read the story himself, so he had no issues yet with the reading assignments.

Second Semester

He was reading picture books, but because he was so smart, he could figure out the story visually and look as if he understood what he was reading, when in fact he wasn't decoding all the words. It fooled us for a while. Later, when we met with the director of the Dyslexia school, she explained this concept to us. It is actually a common coping mechanism for Dyslexic kids. They use the pictures and other clues from the story to help them figure words out. Because they are smart, they can understand the story without actually being able to read all the words. She also explained, however, that, as he advanced through the grades at school, he would be less able to rely on this coping mechanism. If we hadn't been lucky enough to get help early, we surely would have noted problems later when the reading became more complex.

Third Semester
- Could identify uppercase and lowercase letters
- Understood concepts of rhyming
- Connected letter sounds to the symbol
- Distinguished sounds within words
- Could do sound blending easily
- Enjoyed looking at books and listening to stories
- Could retell a story
- Developed word matching
- Could identify sight words

Just by looking at the grid part of his report card, he got all twos and threes. A two meant "developing appropriately," and a three meant "consistently demonstrated."

This would imply he was doing great in reading and had no issues. But if you actually read the report card, the teacher's note is where the first clue appears. The teacher stated that "Félix-Alexander continued to work hard and made progress this term, but his current reading level is below grade level."

In addition, the teacher was sending home a list of practice skills to do over the summer. This makes sense, as now he actually had to read every word in the book. He could no longer just listen to a story or look at pictures for clues.

Where have your child's report cards seemed to contradict themselves? Look over teachers' comments and see if there are any clues to Dyslexia to help you find it early and get the help your child needs.

Sight Words

Every day, we practiced the sight words at home. So these words he mastered. Where he was running into difficulties was when he was learning something new and did not have time to practice in advance in regards to reading.

Social and Work Skills

Even in kindergarten, teachers enjoyed having Félix-Alexander as a student. He's a very caring and engaged student. He's also a hard worker and gets along very well with his classmates. And he's always respectful of others. He was a wonderful student and still is today. His eagerness to learn is infectious, and it shows in all he does.

Five to Six Years Old (First Grade)

Following are comments from the teachers taken directly from my son's report cards. My goal is to show you, the reader, a true and accurate view of being a Dyslexic, and mostly to inspire you with our story so you can also see that there's always hope.

Writing Skills and Motor Skills

- "Félix has improved greatly in his writing this year, but still struggles to write certain letters of the alphabet. Félix's strength lies in his boundless curiosity and unique ideas. The challenge is getting all of this on the pages of his writing journal."

- "Félix has a lot of passion about certain subjects and uses them in his writing."
- "His knowledge and love of story were strong, yet his writing skills prevented him from moving forward at the same pace as his peers. During the editing process, we decided to type Félix's story because rewriting his work was an extremely laborious process for him. This helped eliminate some of the frustration during writer's workshop."

Reading

- "One of Félix's strengths is **persistence**. If he can't decode the word, he seeks assistance right away by saying, 'Excuse me. What sound do *t* and *h* make together?' When Félix is reading, he doesn't skip the words or guess them; you can hear him sounding out every single letter/sound. He even uses the strategy of covering part of the word with his finger in order to sound out the word. Félix knows the long and short sounds for all the letters. However, he does not yet read independently the consonant digraphs like *sh* and *th*. This keeps him from blending the sounds together and reading the word."
- "Since September, Félix has achieved incredibly high results in reading because of his consistent one-on-one support at home and school. However, he still is in his own reading group, has a challenging time reading directions in other subjects like math, Spanish, or music, and needs constant support." (January report card)
- "When Félix reads picture books, he needs to look at pictures first and then attack the text."
- "It is also very important to stop him and talk about the events and characters to make sure he is not only decoding, but also comprehending the text."

- "If in September Félix needed to be reminded to focus on his book during silent reading, in June he couldn't put the book away. Félix doesn't have any problem choosing a book to read and spending thirty minutes reading it. He never skips the words he can't decode. When he finds the one he can't read, he will ask his friend or a teacher for help." (June report card)

Social Skills/Work Habits/Study Skills

- "Félix is a very self-aware young boy."
- "Félix has a lot of friends in his classroom. This semester so many students say, 'Félix is my best friend.'"
- "Félix is the youngest first-grader in our group, which is causing difficulty for Félix with regards to maintaining focus during lessons. However, he is a very positive, motivated, and thoughtful student who excels with homework and offers unique insights during many lessons."

Listening and Speaking

- "Félix is respectful toward others during discussion. He has trouble doing more than one thing at once." (Example: drawing while listening to a story)
- "Félix expresses very creative ideas consistently and asks thoughtful questions."
- "He is extremely curious."
- "One of Félix's biggest achievements during the second part of the school year was becoming an active listener. It is so obvious when Félix is listening and when not. When he is an active listener, you can see that from his face expression and constant questions, like "What does that word mean?"

or "Why did Omri get angry at his brother?" He became one of the students who would ask to continue reading the novel even if it was time to go home. Félix loves aloud readings and discussions."

Mathematics

- "Félix really enjoys math. If he is given a choice, he always picks math. He has made very strong progress in just four months. In the beginning of the year, Félix couldn't skip count by twos, fives, or tens. **He used to get frustrated by consistent trouble with reading directions**, and he didn't have an understanding of telling time or recognizing and counting money. However, now he needs to be slowed down when he is skip counting. Without any challenges, he recognizes the coins and shows time to half an hour."

- "One of Félix's strengths is his ability to use learned strategies, like adding doubles and manipulatives like base ten blocks and number charts."

- "Félix's interest in technology, like calculators and computers, enhances his skills in math."

- "Félix is a strong math student. When he is working by himself **and knows the directions,** he is very productive and successful."

- "When Félix approaches a problem he can't solve, he gets the number grid, coins, or clock and solves it. In addition, he has a very good memory."

- "He remembers his facts and strategies learned in previous lessons."

- "I would highly recommend **practicing basic addition and subtraction facts, counting money and making change, telling and writing time during the summer.**"

Science

- "Félix was unbelievable during every single theme lesson. This boy loves science! He loves researching and recording his findings about habitats, animals, and use of his river, the Ob. In addition, Félix was very creative making the model of his river and favorite animal. During theme night, he blew everyone away as the Ob River expert."

> I have purposely put clues to Dyslexia in bold so the illustration is clear. Now that you see them in my son's report card, review your child's report card. Are there clues there that need to be investigated further? Could an apparent difficulty in math actually be caused by your child's difficulty in reading the instructions? Could Dyslexia be the explanation?

Following are comments from the teachers taken directly from my son's report cards. My goal is to show you, the reader, a true and accurate view of being a Dyslexic, and mostly to inspire you with our story so you can also see that there's always hope.

Speech

We were concerned about FéZander's speech, as sometimes it would be hard to understand him. He didn't always articulate clearly. Since we wanted to help him as soon as possible, we had him evaluated by a professional speech therapist. The therapist reassured us and told us it was developmental and would go away on its own by ages eight to ten. By the way, his lisp never fully resolved on its own, so now we are in private speech therapy (more on this subject to come in later chapters).

At least two of his teachers told us that Félix was an incredible student and the best they ever had (even to this day). Another said he was one of the most caring students he'd ever had, and others' comments were "Thank you for sharing him with us. He's awesome."

When he was given the instructions verbally, he could accomplish anything. But he would run into problems when he had to read the instructions himself, then answer the question.

For example, he loves and excels in math, but if he had to read and understand the question by himself, he would get lost and not complete the assignment on time. This wasn't because of a difficulty with the math concept. Rather, it was his inability to read the directions that would cause the issue.

There are two different distinctions here that are very important:

1. This could have led the teacher to assume he didn't understand math when he actually excelled at it.
2. It could have hurt his self-esteem because if this issue had not been caught early, he might have come to the conclusion that he was not good in math.

My Observations in Reviewing This Information
Reading

- Loved and understood "read alouds." When someone else read the story aloud, he had no issues retaining and understanding the concepts in the books.
- Enjoyed verbal discussions about a book but had difficulty writing ideas on paper.
- Could easily piece together the meaning of the story when pictures were included in the book. He looked at the picture first, then read the story.

- Very smart, so he could easily decode enough words to piece the story together without necessarily being able to read all the words. This is hard to detect early on and will cause issues later on, as reading difficulties will be detected much later when reading comprehension is necessary for school assignments.

Sight Words/Math
- Practiced daily at home, so he did okay, but in class he sometimes had difficulties completing assignments.

Motor Skills/Writing
- Difficulty forming letters and numbers.
- Tired easily and could not always complete written work on time. This is where words like "lazy," "unmotivated," "unfocused," "defiant," "lack of effort," "inconsistency," etc. can come into play.
- Great ideas, very creative, but couldn't get them on paper. Writing was laborious.
- Difficulties with doing two things at once (couldn't write and listen at same time).

Mathematics
- Difficulties with basic math facts, but awesome at solving complex math problems. (Einstein had the same difficulty in his early childhood.) Extremely good in math with strategies and comprehension, but needed to practice math facts.
- Really good in math when given oral instructions, but finishing work on time when he needed to read the instructions by himself was more difficult. It was not a lack of math comprehension. It was because reading the instructions prevented him from understanding the problem to be solved.

- Needed more time to complete tests. Knew the answers but couldn't finish on time.

Miscellaneous

- Very talented in some subjects (science) while struggling in others (writing).
- Attention: seemed distracted, unfocused, inattentive, and uncooperative, when in fact he was disoriented, struggling, tired, frustrated, etc.
- Technologies like computers are greatly helpful in alleviating the stress and frustration for the student and the teachers.
- Speech articulation issues, lisp.
- Dyslexics are known to have difficulties with lapsed time and difficulty telling time.
- Positive words associated with Dyslexics:
    - Have very unique and creative ideas
    - Are insightful
    - Are persistent
    - Are hard workers
    - Are caring friends and students

"The Second Time Around, We Caught It Early!" in Summary for the Right-Brain Thinker and Dyslexic

Below are examples of the signs of Dyslexia FéZander experienced:

- **Speech**
    - Lisp and articulation

- **Reading**
  - Decoding difficulties
  - Reading aloud is challenging.
  - Would get frustrated when he had trouble reading directions
  - When given directions verbally, he could do the assignment, but if he had to read the directions, he had difficulty doing the task.
- **Motor Skills**
  - Difficulty forming letters and numbers
  - Tired easily when writing
  - Difficulty writing and listening at the same time
  - Difficulty putting ideas on paper
  - Laborious writing (computers are a great help and relief)
- **Math**
  - Math facts and timed tests took hard work to master.
- **Spelling** (one aspect that may linger longer)
  - Pretest scores were sometimes low, and test scores were always much higher as he had TIME to practice during the week. Needs time!
- **Focus/Concentration**
  - He had difficulty staying focused for long periods of time.
  - He could be fidgety.

Following are FéZander's strengths and some of the reasons HE overcame Dyslexia. Where is your child similar? Where can you help him develop these characteristics more?

- He NEVER gives up.
- His eagerness to learn is infectious.
- He has a positive attitude.
- He's a very hard worker.
- He gets along well with his classmates and friends.
- He's got a boundless curiosity and unique ideas.
- He's got a wealth of knowledge in many subjects.
- He's persistent.
- He loves to read.
- He's very self-aware.
- He loves school.
- He seeks assistance when needed.
- He utilizes and applies the strategies he learned in remedial reading classes.
- He studies and practices consistently.
- He wants to succeed.
- He enjoys, understands, and excels with technologies (computers, calculators, phones, etc.).
- He is a strong math student (even when he had difficulties with math facts).
- He has a great memory.
- He LOVES science!
- He is very creative.

CHAPTER 8

Let's Fix This!

By May of first grade, we had gathered enough evidence to see that something was going on with our son academically. At this point, we still were unsure what was happening and how to take care of it, but we knew FéZander needed help somehow. By now, teachers were really concerned because our son had difficulties reading at grade level even though it was obvious he was very smart. And his writing was laborious compared to the other, older kids in his classroom.

For us, another important factor that became key was when our daughter, who is twenty-one months younger than our son, started to read around the age of three. This was right around the time our son was having difficulties with reading. Imagine our surprise when we saw this little girl reading like crazy when we had been struggling for years with our son. It was like night and day, so much so that we thought she was memorizing the books, as she was that good. Turns out, she was incredibly gifted in reading and still is today. She was reading chapter books on her own by four years of age.

The contrast was shocking and an eye-opener for us. This was yet another blessing in our life, as it helped us see that our son needed help as soon as possible.

> Do you have a similar intuition that a contrast between your child's reading and his peers might have something to do with Dyslexia? Trust that feeling and look into it more thoroughly. You will be glad you did.

This was a great lesson for us as parents. You can be a brilliant pediatrician, caring nurse, and a successful business owner and still lose complete perspective when it comes to your kids. It's much easier to assess other people's problems and help them out than it is to help yourself and your kids. It's hard to see solutions to problems when you are stuck in the middle of them. It's only when you can step back and look at the whole picture that the solutions come. This is the moment when our journey into helping our son with his reading difficulties really began.

Not realizing there were different kinds of remedial reading classes and not knowing what FéZander actually needed in terms of reading assistance, we enrolled him in a basic remedial reading class. Within a few weeks, we realized that these classes were more designed to help kids who needed to catch up on the school curriculum than to help them decode the words. FéZander attended the reading classes after school three or four times a week for one hour each time. It would be set up with about two or three kids per teacher, and each day they would work on a specific lesson. First, the kids got assessed in their reading capabilities. Then they were assigned to a specific curriculum (kindergarten, first grade, second grade, and so on) and a teacher. Students worked in groups, and each group studied the same curriculum. As months passed, we came to find out that this type of remedial class is great for kids who need to catch up but is not geared towards Dyslexics. For example, these classes are helpful for kids who are learning English as a second language, who just moved from another country, or who just need extra help, but are not designed to help kids with decoding difficulties, like Dyslexics. At the time, we still didn't know our son was Dyslexic, but we knew the classes weren't working out.

After two months and not much improvement in our son's reading capabilities, we started asking around for other solutions. Eventually someone gave us the name of this amazing remedial school that was geared towards Dyslexics. We figured we'd try it out. Even though we weren't sure he was Dyslexic, we figured one-on-one tutoring would be better than what we were doing at that moment. We called the school and begged to be seen. They were so busy that we were on a waiting list. We kept calling, and within a few weeks, they hired a new teacher, so they took us in. We had found our home! Within two months of one-on-one lessons, our son went from kindergarten reading to second-grade level. It was incredible! This is where we really started connecting the dots and finally figured out he was actually Dyslexic.

For four years, my son attended this school. He went twice a week during the school year and twenty sessions in the summers. They worked on every subject with which he needed help, like reading, decoding words, spelling, grammar rules, writing, and on and on. He loved going to his lessons and enjoyed his teacher tremendously. We still keep in contact today. She was a great teacher and confidante for my son, and we'll forever be grateful for all she did for our FéZander.

"Let's Fix This!" in Summary for
the Right-Brain Thinker and Dyslexic

- **Reading classes**: Not all remedial reading classes are equal and helpful for Dyslexics. Dyslexics learn and process information differently, so they need a different approach to learning how to read. Traditional reading lessons are designed to help children catch up on their reading skills. Specialized classes for Dyslexia teach kids how to read by addressing their decoding difficulties.

- Get help as soon as you recognize the signs of Dyslexia. Check out our website **DyslexicAndUnStoppable.com,** as we have tons of useful and user-friendly information for parents. E-mail us with questions, and we'll do our best to help you.

- Patience and positive reinforcement are crucial to your child's self-esteem. Your child is trying his hardest and needs your support and encouragement.

- There isn't any quick-fix cure for Dyslexia. It will be hard work for you and especially for your child, but the results are worth the effort. Take it one step at a time and one day at a time, and you'll be amazed to see what your child can accomplish. The key is consistency and perseverance.

- Focus on your child's talents rather than his weaknesses to empower him every day.

FéZander summer of 2012
(on vacation in Nantucket)

- Be your child's advocate, and learn the signs of Dyslexia. Following are some difficulties encountered by Dyslexic children:
  - Reading aloud
  - Decoding words
  - Learning spelling words
  - Memorizing basic math facts and timed tests
  - Laborious handwriting
  - Mixing uppercase and lowercase when writing
  - Remembering the alphabet
  - Speech issues
  - Fidgetiness
  - Fine motor skills
  - Learning to tell time
- Keep the lines of communications between you and the teachers open, honest, and positive for your child's sake. **Don't blame anyone; it's unhelpful and won't fix the problem.** Stay focused on solutions!
- Collaboration with the teachers is critical. But remember, as parents, *we* are responsible for our kids, not the teachers. Teachers are great allies and are a wonderful support system. But ultimately, *we* are responsible for our own kids and their success in life!
- Associate with like-minded people and join mastermind groups. As a parent of a Dyslexic child, you also need help and support on this journey. The parents require as much love and encouragement as the children to maintain focus and persevere.

CHAPTER 9

The Right Tools at the Right Time!

Second Grade

By the time second grade started, we had only had a few months at the new reading school. So even though FéZander had made tremendous strides in reading, he still had plenty of work to do. Luckily, we had a great and understanding teacher who wanted to help our son succeed. So we had a great year.

The biggest challenges that year were:

Math Facts

In second grade, even though FéZander knew his basic math facts, he had difficulties on tests because the goal was to answer as many questions as possible in the least amount of time. Kids were timed on how fast they could answer math questions on a test. It was all about speed, and Dyslexia is simply NOT. Wow! That was one serious challenge for us. FéZander felt the pressure, as Dyslexics have great difficulty with timed assignments. That was a really big stressor and took years to master. To this day, we still practice math facts to stay as sharp and fast as possible.

Focus, Concentration, Organization, and Spelling

These areas still needed improving.

Writing (Punctuation and Organization)

In this area, FéZander again had creative ideas and great imagination but still needed help organizing his thoughts on paper. What we did was to set up a collaboration between his school teacher and his reading teacher. They would simultaneously work on the current lessons. FéZander would bring his spelling words and essays with him to reading classes, and those assignments would be incorporated into the weekly lesson. It was a great partnership, and FéZander's success was showing up in all areas of his schooling.

Speech

Even though FéZander's speech difficulties remained present, since they didn't affect his performance, grades, and results in school, he didn't qualify for formal speech therapy. As a consequence, he received only a few speech therapy lessons here and there during that year with minimal success.

 Key point: If you can, set up an alliance with your child's teacher. Incorporate any outside professionals you may use. Help them all to collaborate to maximize your child's learning experience.

Third Grade

By third grade, FéZander had been in his specialized reading classes for about 1½ years, and it showed.

He was making tremendous strides in reading, writing, and math facts testing. Our system was set up and was working smoothly because we had a collaboration between the teachers (regular school teacher and reading school teacher) who were coordinating lessons.

Below are comments from the teacher on his report card:

- "Félix is adjusting nicely to third grade. He is working hard and making good progress. In reading, Félix can give a good oral and written summary of a book that he is reading."
- "Félix has good ideas for writing, and he is creating some wonderful stories."
- "Félix understands all math concepts taught this term."
- "Félix is working on staying focused and organizing himself this term."
- "He enjoyed being in book clubs this term and had wonderful discussions with his group."
- "He was fluent in his math facts."
- "It was wonderful to have you in our class this year!"
- "He is a joy to have in our classroom."
- "He understands what he is reading and can have a good oral discussion of the book."
- "Awesome work, Félix."

Some persistent difficulties were:

- "Félix has good ideas for writing but sometimes has a difficult time getting his ideas written."

- "Please continue to read and practice math facts over the summer."

Fourth Grade

By fourth grade, FéZander was still going to the remedial reading classes twice a week and twenty times during the summer. And year by year, his hard work paid off immensely. My kid is one DETERMINED boy who never gives up! Love him and his perseverance.

Following are a few more comments on his report cards in fourth grade to show you the great progress he made. Most importantly, I show you these comments so you can see what is possible and dare to hope!

- "I am especially pleased with his efforts in studying his weekly spelling words and test scores."
- "I'm extremely proud of Félix's Native American board game. It was well planned, designed, informative, fun to play, and a great team project!"
- "Félix puts forth genuine effort and continues to do well academically."
- "I am proud of his accomplishments in reading with including more text evidence when answering reading comprehension questions."
- "I am proud of Félix with his math accomplishments, especially learning his multiplication and division facts."
- "He did a fantastic job of writing very detailed and informative research reports and produced two impressive PowerPoint slide shows."
- "Felix, have a great summer. I'll miss you."

Some persistent difficulties were:

- "Please have Félix review his elapsed time and two-digit by two-digit multiplication steps and his expository writing sample over the summer to keep his academic skills active."

The summer just before fifth grade started, FéZander officially graduated from his remedial reading classes. Congrats, my boy!

He worked so very hard and deserves all the praises in the world. He accomplished all of this success by himself with determination and perseverance! NO one could do the work but him, and he was incredibly dedicated and changed his life forever! The sky is not the limit for this kid. Nothing is! He's truly UN-Stoppable.

Fifth Grade

At the end of fourth grade, FéZander graduated from elementary school and was now attending fifth grade in a new private school.

He's thriving and enjoying every minute of being at his new school. He loves every subject, especially science, and does every after-school activity he can possibly fit in his schedule and loves it! If he had more hours in a day, he would want to do more. He was a trumpet player in the school band, did chess club, art classes, woodworking classes, archery, tennis lessons, just to name a few. And, in addition to the after-school activities, he received his black belt in tae kwon do and, on some weekends, also attended computer programming classes.

 Explore your child's different interests. Allow him to pursue sports, the arts, and music to find his passion. This will help him to develop that UN-Stoppable spirit!

Again, here are a few comments from his report cards to show you how well he's doing now that he has completed his remedial reading lessons.

- "Félix is a successful reading student. His comprehension of a more complex novel is strong, and Félix is an eager participant during class. His comments about mature concepts were insightful."
- "Félix demonstrates a love for learning and an ability to make connections throughout the curriculum."

** Just those few comments from the teachers are worth all the money we spent on remedial reading classes and all the countless hours FéZander spent working hard. IT JUST WORKS!

- "Félix is conscientious and hardworking, and his work represents this."
- "Félix becomes very focused and serious when doing math problems. His performance has been solid, and he is developing a strong foundation with the skills and concepts taught this term."
- "He knows all his facts quickly and correctly." **Yes, success!**
- "Félix is an enthusiastic student, and he loves the study of history. In addition, Félix is highly motivated and always puts forth his best effort on all assignments."
- "During class discussions, Félix is a strong and eager participant. His answers to challenging questions reflect his ability to think critically about more sophisticated topics."
- "Félix is a wonderful student to have in class! His positive attitude and strong work ethic should be commended. Félix, this is an impressive report!"

- "What a delight he is!"
- "Félix remains enthusiastic and committed to his science learning. He is a daily contributor to discussions and an active learner during investigations. Félix's quiz scores are evidence of the level of understanding that he commands."
- "Félix is a pleasure to have in class."
- "His genuine interest in the subject matter was obvious. His enthusiasm was often contagious, and he continued to share his knowledge and love of learning with the other children."
- "Félix continued to be highly motivated, and his calm and considerate manner made him an excellent team player."
- "Félix continued his success in reading during the second semester. Although the choice of novels was more challenging in nature, Félix's comprehension skills continued to be superior. His interesting connections about more mature topics reflected both his intelligence and the wealth of knowledge he has on various subjects."
- "Félix has had a successful year in science. Félix has been a dependable team member when it came to group work, and both parties won when he was involved. His progress and effort were evident all year."
- "As the year progressed, he became more confident while making an effort to work neatly. His final art painting of fish was so original and a perfect way for Félix to end the year."
- "Félix has performed well this semester. He has demonstrated noticeable improvement with all his physical skills and knowledge of the activities we introduced in class. Félix worked very hard during the fitness portion of class."

Difficulties that will remain part of FéZander's life and won't EVER stop him:

- "The mechanics of writing are difficult for Félix. As a goal for next semester, I would like Félix to use the computer to complete written assignments." (YES, THANK YOU for computers!)
- "He works very hard to learn the sports we have introduced in class. Félix does need to keep working and practicing his manipulative skills."
- "Keyboarding will help Félix complete his work in an organized manner."
- "Félix's second-semester grade reveals some inconsistencies in his efforts concerning assignments." (This is an example where complex spelling was involved.) Later, when we had a chance to sit down and talk about this test, FéZander told me, 'I just could not get the words to stay in my head.' (This is a spelling difficulty, not a lack-of-effort incident. FéZander is okay with it and understands that as long as he tries his best, that's all that matters in the end.) More later on this subject (spelling and "lack of effort").

Speech

By the end of fifth grade, FéZander still had a noticeable lisp. So we are now pursuing one-on-one private speech therapy. Within a few lessons, we will be able to fix this glitch as soon as possible and move on to bigger and better things in life, like his passion for "saving the endangered sharks."

We purposely included in the book those challenges that remain present because we want to give you the whole picture. Challenges will continue for your child and mine throughout their lives. The key is to arm them with the UN-Stoppable spirit to overcome all of them!

"The Right Tools at the Right Time!" in Summary for the Right-Brain Thinker and Dyslexic

- Proper reading classes bring great success in reading.
- Early intervention removes frustrations and improves self-esteem.
- Focus on your child's strengths. Pick your battles wisely, and save your energy for positive interactions and interventions.
- Don't dwell on your child's weaknesses or compare him to others, but rather, find his talents and focus on finding his niche. Every one of us has talents and faces challenges in life.
- Try your best and move on. For example, spelling difficulties will probably remain a challenge for FéZander, and he's okay with it. As long as he tries his best, that's all that matters.
- Do make sure the teachers are aware of your child's specific challenges so they don't label him as having "lack of effort" or as having "inconsistencies" in his assignments.
- Work hard five to six days a week, and play hard on your rest day. Dyslexics don't have the luxury of taking the whole summer off from academic homework. So reward them with quality time off on rest days.
- Use computer technologies as much as possible to do written and reading assignments (spell-check, Dragon Dictation, audiobooks, etc.). Focus on the quality of their work, not the quantity.

- Practice math facts daily for short periods of time instead of infrequent and long periods.
- Consistency is the key. Ten minutes daily five or six days a weeks is more productive than one hour periodically.
- Reward your child positively. Dyslexics work super hard and deserve recognition.
- Math facts can remain an issue because of the timing and speed. As long as the teacher can differentiate between not knowing the facts and not doing them fast enough, then the student has a better chance of success. And in our case, the teacher was able to recognize that FéZander excelled in math, even when he had difficulties in timed math fact tests. She still put him in the advanced math group, and he continued to excel.
- Placement on the paper and alignment are often the reason for errors on FéZander's math problems—not because he doesn't know the answer, but because he doesn't align the numbers correctly and loses track of where he is.
- Learning elapsed time: By nature, because Dyslexia is a glitch in the processing of information, it makes it more difficult for students to understand the concept of time perception.

CHAPTER 10

Observations We've Made Along This Journey

FéZander Will Try Anything

Being Dyslexic has no boundaries, in my son's view. He is always willing to try anything. A new sport, a new game, a difficult challenge, or a scary obstacle is always welcomed. FéZander never turns down an opportunity to grow and to learn new things.

FéZander Is a Philanthropist and Animal Lover

In third grade, FéZander came to us and said: "For my birthday, I do not want presents. Instead, I want to raise money to save the endangered sharks." He raised $610.25 and sent it all to *Sharkwater* when he was only eight years old. He now has a nonprofit website and raises awareness about sharks as much as he can. FéZander is very empathetic, and he has a lot of compassion for animals. I'm always amazed to see how understanding of others and their feelings he is. I work on nurturing this beautiful quality in him, as it is a gift. He also loves dogs and would have twenty-five of them if only his parents would allow him!

FéZander Has Big Dreams, Big Vision

For as long as I can remember, FéZander has talked about all the jobs he will do when he grows up. Most of them are to help animals, our planet, and make this world a better place for mankind. Since the age of four, he's been writing engineering journals.

These journals are filled with designs and ideas of machines he will build as he gets older. For example, one machine is to help the miners so they do not have to go underground anymore (like the drone airplanes for the air force). He would like to replace humans with machines to keep them safe on land instead of being put in dangerous jobs in tunnels underground.

FéZander Is Reserved and Quiet

Since FéZander was born, he has always enjoyed spending time by himself, playing and creating. And since the day he started day care, teachers have come to us with the concern that he sometimes plays by himself. Every year since he was eighteen months old, we've had the same conversation with teachers, and the outcome afterward has always been the same. This is just who FéZander is! Sometimes he likes to play by himself, and other times he wants to play with his friends. Sometimes he can be very quiet, and other times he is VERY loud. Each time we sat with the teachers, we helped them see that when FéZander is playing by himself on the playground, he's happy, content, and satisfied. He is not upset, crying, or sad. He is just one of those kids who needs space to be creative. He is not antisocial or unfriendly, but rather, creative and independent. These are two different things. Great teachers see this distinction, but some don't, and we suspect it is just part of the society we live in today. When

FéZander feels like playing with his friends, he does; when he feels like being creative and playing in his mind or by himself, he does. That's it, end of story! There's no big mystery to solve here.

 Nurture the introvert in your child. Of course you want your child to have friends and socialize. He also needs time to be by himself, invent new games, and plan for the future.

I notice that this society seems scared and misinformed about the meaning of the word *introvert*. It's a good thing to be an introvert. Many introverts are the brilliant ones who create fabulous inventions and technologies in this world. These great people with amazing imaginations need time and space to think. They can't always be on a "normal" schedule (soccer, tennis, lacrosse, hockey, piano lessons, ballet, and dance lessons, all in one week). To be creative and innovative takes time, energy, quiet spaces, and healthy environments.

For some reason, this modern society seems apprehensive towards introverts. Introverts constantly put themselves outside of their comfort zone just to fit in, even when it goes against every fiber of their being. Why? We need a balance of both introverts and extroverts in this world. It's time to reconsider this idea, because if you are consistently on the go, socializing, playing computer games, etc., when can you find the time to create something amazing? Creators and inventors need space to think, as it takes time and discipline to create and be innovative. Most importantly, after spending a few weeks with my son, teachers realize how cool he is and that he is having fun with or without his friends.

I may not completely change people's minds about introverts, but at least I know my kid is COOL and AWESOME!

FéZander the Engineer!

Since the age of four, FéZander has been writing engineering design journals.

Anyone who spends quality time talking with my son realizes that he's got an "engineer brain." From the moment he wakes up until the time he goes to bed, all he talks about is how does this work, why is this like that, can I open this gadget and see how it works inside? He wants to know!

His playroom is a mix of Legos (thousands and thousands of Legos), science experiments, and old parts and pieces of dismantled machines. That's what makes him the happiest, figuring how things work. Do you think that the fact that he is not the fastest to answer the math facts quiz matters? Of course not. He still is able to figure complex math and science problems that even adults don't understand. He comes home annoyed on days when field trips are scheduled on Fridays, as he misses science class.

He loves field trips, but he also loves science. He doesn't understand why many kids don't get or like science; he would eat it for breakfast if he could!

When we did the IQ testing with my son, he was afraid to be told he wasn't Dyslexic because if he weren't, then in his mind it would mean that he wasn't actually as smart and creative as he was told. That was a big concern to him. Go figure. Hoping to be Dyslexic, now that's something! Not wanting to just be "normal."

You have the power to make your child's life fantastic. So DO IT! Let him be who he is. Who cares about being so-called normal? Let him find his strengths to be great and unique. It's what makes life fun, interesting, challenging, and worth living. I dare you to be yourself and be unique!

My son's first memorable word was, without a doubt, *why*. I know it's normal for kids to ask why, but my kid is by far the most inquisitive kid I know. He just wants to know and understand how life works. That's a beautiful character strength to see. He cares about the environment he lives in. He cares about the people who surround him. He cares about the well-being of the animals in the world. From the tiniest little bug to the gigantic great white shark, he wants to do all he can to protect them. He's always inquiring about life and looking to understand how things work. He's an "old soul" in a ten-year-old's body, as one of my friends calls him. His wisdom is greater than most, and his commitment to humanity is remarkable.

FéZander and Sports

Yesterday was a particularly hard day for me as a parent and as a Dyslexic because the harsh realities of having Dyslexia sometimes creep up in sports. I see my son work so much harder than other kids to learn techniques and skills, and they don't always come easy for him. Some days are better than others, but what gets me is the lack of recognition he sometimes gets.

It was fascinating to see how a few people assumed that when FéZander got his black belt in tae kwon do, he would simply quit. Maybe they thought that because he's not a "star" that he would give up. What they truly don't understand about FéZander is that he loves tae kwon do, and he's more determined and perseverant than most kids. The biggest mistake I see people doing when they judge us, the Dyslexics, is they "**UNDER**ESTIMATE" us tremendously.

My first reaction in a situation like this is for me to get angry and be hurt. But eventually, I come to realize that once again these comments have ***nothing*** to do with me or my kids. They are all projections dumped on us. It has ***nothing*** to do with us and everything to do with that person's own insecurities.

So eventually, I let it go, and I start to giggle as I get a warm and happy feeling inside and think, "Thank you again for giving me renewed energy and fuel to keep going on this journey."

The art of practicing tae kwon do is a lot more about conquering your fears and having fierce determination than being a star athlete. Thank you Master Han, for seeing the best in my family and always helping us on this journey. Your willingness to help us succeed is remarkable and truly appreciated.

Some people think that with more discipline and a regimented workout and tough critique, the Dyslexic child is going to perform better! NO, no, no, and NO! Our kids need love, understanding, and kind, compassionate, and meaningful praise. We want to encourage our kids, not discourage them. Rewarding them for their efforts and their tenacity to still keep going even when they find it challenging will help them be UN-Stoppable. It's just so painful as a parent to live in a society that is focused on *performance*. What about determination and perseverance, even if you are not the best at that sport? In my opinion, as long as my kid likes going to his practices and enjoys doing the sport, I think that's all that really matters in the end. Let's face it. Most kids are not going to become professionals in sports, even when they are very good. So why not just enjoy the camaraderie of the sport instead of constantly competing?

My son is passionate about all he undertakes, including sports. He enjoys collaborating and being part of a team. But mostly, he enjoys spending time socializing and hanging out with his friends. Just by observing him, people don't realize that he tries a thousand times harder than some other kids, and he's more committed than most.

In our family, we do not force our kids to do any sports. They choose to be there because they enjoy the sport. And on a few occasions, I've noticed people assuming he was just not trying hard enough. It breaks my heart! It crushes my spirit, and then I need time to recuperate, as I find it too painful to bear sometimes.

But then again, I come home and have a conversation with my kid about what just happened and I find out he's okay. He's the one comforting me and telling me all is fine. FéZander has this remarkable ability to let comments just glide down his back, and he just keeps on going. He gives ME hope again. He's truly an amazing and incredible human being, and I'm so lucky and fortunate to be his mom. He's such a gift! Thank you, thank you! I tell him all the time, I wouldn't ever want to change a thing about him; he's perfect just as he IS!

> Become a strong advocate for your child. Support him in his interests. Even if he is not the best in a sport, as long as he enjoys it, encourage him to stick with it. This perseverance will teach him to be UN-Stoppable.

As I was writing this book, my son was in school, and one day he came to me with a test result that needed my signature. (Not good, right?) His score was low, and I was really surprised since it was a subject he really enjoys. The assignment was to match the words with the definitions. Anyway, I asked him what had happened, and he said: "I did study, and as I was studying, I just could not memorize the words. They would not stay in my head." Right away I knew it was part of being Dyslexic, since I know he always tries his best, does his homework on time, and studies every day. And most importantly, he enjoys school and that subject. So, without judgment or anger, I asked him to promise me that next time this happens that he will come to me right away so I can help him decode the words. My whole point for this anecdote is to show you that a teacher could easily see this test result and think he was lazy and did not study, when in fact he actually tried very hard to learn the words, as he's a determined and hardworking student. This is why you need great communication with the teachers and why they need to know your child, so that they have an accurate response to the situation arising. This way, the problem gets addressed as soon as possible, and your child gets a better chance of succeeding.

This situation made me realize I needed to write a letter to give to the teachers as we navigate through the school years. Each year we have to start over in a new grade with new teachers who are not always aware of the circumstances of every single child in the classroom. I do not want to give out the letter to each teacher right at the start of the school year, as Dyslexia is not an obstacle in my child's life. And most importantly, I don't ever want his teachers to label him and not expect as much from him. But I think it is a great tool to present to the teacher when a situation arises so that the teacher understands where my child is coming from and what's going on in a particular circumstance. This way, the teacher can see my child with a clear vision and be more tolerant and patient with him if he's having difficulties with a task or subject. I think some subjects, like language arts and foreign language courses with spelling words and writing assignments, will always be a bit difficult for my son, and that's okay. As long as a child tries his best, what more can a parent and teacher expect? In my opinion, the effort and enthusiasm my son brings to the class surely make up for the fact that he makes a few spelling errors here and there.

In fact, FéZander crafted a letter to his teacher.

Félix-Alexander Clarkson Curtiss

Dear Teacher:

I would like to start this school year by introducing myself to all my teachers. My first name is Félix-Alexander. My friends call me Félix, and my parents and my sister call me Baba or FéZander. As you can see, I have many nicknames, and I like them all.

Since we'll be spending a whole year together, I thought this year I would try something different and introduce myself ahead of time so that by the time school starts, you have a great picture in your head of who I am. I had an amazing experience at H.H. (Hamden Hall) last year and look forward to another fabulous one in sixth grade. H.H. is so awesome, and I feel at home here! I'm glad to be a student at this great school!

I LOVE going to school. I'm very passionate and eager to learn. I am fascinated by science and the world, so I'm always reading about these subjects. This makes me resourceful and very knowledgeable for my young age. (My mom calls me Baba.com like Google.com.) I'm always sad when the end of year comes, because I truly enjoy school.

In kindergarten and first grade, I had difficulties with reading and spelling, so my parents investigated the situation and found out I'm actually Dyslexic. For four years, (from summer of first grade to the beginning of fifth grade) I went to the Learning House in Guilford to help me with reading.

I was truly one of the lucky ones. We found out I was Dyslexic early, and I spent the next four years getting one-on-one tutoring in reading. I went twice a week every week during the school year and twenty sessions each summer. I worked really hard, and it paid off. Now I'm a great reader, and I love it. By the beginning of fifth grade, I had a tenth grade comprehension in reading.

I'm Dyslexic and UN-Stoppable! Dyslexia doesn't ever stop me, and I'm actually proud of it. I'm very creative, super smart, and I have great ideas. (If you are interested to see, H.H. has a copy of my IQ test, which shows how smart I am.)

When I grow up, I will have many jobs. But my biggest passion is engineering. I love inventing machines and figuring how things works. I have a room designated just for making Lego creations, and I also enjoy taking things apart to see how they work inside. Now I'm in the process of building a science lab in my barn. My goal is to go to MIT just like my grandfather did.

I'm a philanthropist, and I love animals. I have two dogs, one cat, and a bearded dragon. I would love to have twenty-five dogs, but my parents, prefer only two dogs. I created a website to save the endangered sharks. I raised more than six hundred dollars on my eight birthday and gave it to Sharkwater. If you have a moment, go visit my website. It's called www.WorldSharks.com. I'm also in the process of cowriting a book with my parents to help other kids who have Dyslexia and show them they can do anything they put their minds to and be UN-Stoppable. Our book is called Dyslexic and UN-Stoppable.

Getting one-on-one reading instructions remediated my reading issues, so now reading is not a problem, but spelling is sometimes still difficult for me. I just want my teachers to know that I work very hard on all my schoolwork, but sometimes I still struggle with spelling.

Believe me, this is NOT due to a lack of effort. It may appear to you that I'm lacking because of inconsistencies in my test results, but rest assured, lack of effort isn't part of my vocabulary. I try ten times harder and study every day (even during the summers and weekends), but sometimes I still have difficulties with spelling. I want you to know I tried my best, so please be patient with me; I really did my best. I'm brilliant, but unfortunately, I may always struggle with spelling, and I am okay with that, as I know I tried my hardest.

For me, another area I'm struggling with is handwriting. It is very difficult and time-consuming to write with a pen or pencil. I have fabulous ideas, but sometimes I can't write fast enough to capture all my ideas on paper in a specific time frame, like transcribing from the board to my journal. That's why I've been working on computers more and more. It just makes my life so much easier when I can write on computers, as I can type faster than I can form letters. I enjoy writing essays, as I usually can do them on the computer, and you'll get to see how creative I am with my writing; I have great ideas!

I understand that spelling words and language are part of life, so I will continue to try my best.

I know I sometimes fidget in my seat and play with my pencil, but I want you to know, I'm still listening. Always!

Playtime and recess: Sometimes I like to play by myself, and sometimes I like to play with my friends. Sometimes I'm the life of the party, and sometimes I'm very quiet. That's just who I am, and I'm okay with being all those attributes. For example, at recess, when I take time to be by myself, please take a moment and look at me. You'll quickly realize I'm happy; I'm having fun, and I'm content.

You don't need to worry about me when I'm playing by myself. I'm okay, and it's all good. It's just part of who I am. Sometimes I hang out with my best friend for forty-eight hours straight, and sometimes I just enjoy having time by myself to create cool projects. I'm happy in both situations, and I enjoy a blend of both. I like to play with my friends, and I like to create awesome projects.

I'll take a moment to talk about my speech. Since second grade, I've had just a few speech therapy sessions here and there at my old school because I have a lisp. But because it never affected my performance and grades, I never qualified for formal speech therapy in my previous schools. So I would be the last student being helped, which was basically only a few minutes here and there during the three years, I was there. This year, because my parents want the best for me in life, we'll be doing private speech therapy. I'm mentioning it to you because the speech therapist will meet me at school once a week, so you may see us together during the school year. I'm looking forward to the lessons, and the therapist will be able to help me fix my lisp, so I'm very excited. As I said, I'm always willing to try anything and do my best.

I get along great with my teachers, as I'm a nice and caring student, and I truly enjoy school. My teachers are a great source of inspiration for me. I find them very caring and supportive, and I'm truly grateful to have them in my life. Great teachers make all the difference in the world! I hope my introduction letter gives you a great picture of who I am, and I look forward to another fantastic year at H.H., as I love H.H.!

Your student,
FéZander

Another aspect of Dyslexia that brings difficulties to my son's writing is called dysgraphia. Dysgraphia simply means impairment of the ability to write. Following are some of the symptoms of dysgraphia that affect my son's writing capabilities and may affect your child's too:

- Difficulty gripping a pencil comfortably while writing
- Unusual wrist, body, and paper orientations
- Excessive erasures
- Mixed uppercase and lowercase letters
- Inconsistent form and size of letters, or unfinished letters
- Misuse of lines and margins (see picture at right for reference)
- Inefficient speed of copying
- Inattentiveness over details when writing
- Poor legibility
- Handwriting abilities that may interfere with spelling and written composition
- Having a hard time translating ideas to writing, sometimes using the wrong words altogether
- Difficulty spelling words correctly and consistently
- Difficulty aligning numbers correctly while doing math problems
- Difficulty using silverware properly
- Difficulty with buttons and zippers
- Difficulty tying shoes
- Writing and copying are laborious.
- He has a large vocabulary and an impressive book collection.
- Difficulty doing two tasks at once (thinking and writing at the same time)
- The art of writing: (check alignment)
- FéZander works so hard to write that by the time he's done writing a few sentences, he's exhausted and can't think any

longer. His writing doesn't match his ideas. The physical act of writing takes too long. So sometimes he doesn't have time to complete an assignment in class, or it's very messy because he's rushing to get it done on time.

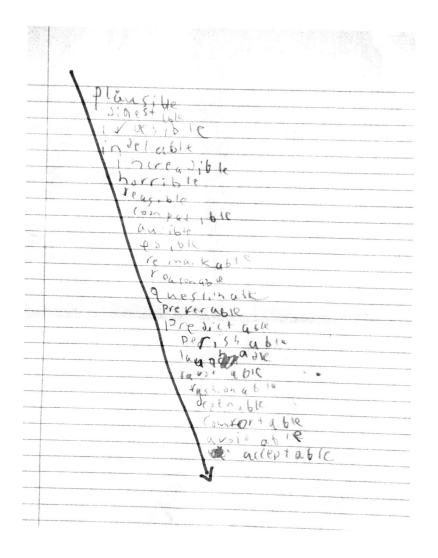

"Observations We've Made along This Journey" in Summary for the Right-Brain Thinker and Dyslexic

- **With Dyslexia comes:** perseverance, compassion, determination and creativity!
- **To create, one needs:** time to think, quiet spaces, self-discipline, introversion, introspection, patience, self-motivation, independence, and an inquisitive mind.
- **Sports:** Sports can be challenging for Dyslexics due to difficulties like:
  - Left- and right-hand coordination
  - Fine motor skills
  - Focusing challenges
  - Competitive nature of sports
- **Roll with it!** Dyslexia is a lifelong condition BUT can successfully be remediated with the right tools and accommodations. Focus on what you are good at doing, and give yourself a break on the rest.
- **Teachers are your allies:** As needed, let your child's teachers know about any lingering challenges so misunderstandings are minimized during the school year. In our case, FéZander still has difficulties with spelling words and fine motor skills. So when his teachers are aware of these challenges, they can better understand and know that he's trying his best. This way, everyone involved is aware of expectations. When teachers understand your child, they can be great resources by offering helpful strategies and accommodations (like computers). Remember, if your teacher doesn't know, how can he help?

- **With Dyslexia** may come:
    - Dysgraphia (writing difficulties)
    - Dyspraxia (speech and/or coordination difficulties)
    - Dyscalculia (math difficulties)

CHAPTER 11

Dear Teachers

This part of my book is written with teachers in mind. In this section, my goal is to bring awareness to teachers, educators, instructors, coaches, mentors, etc. who come in contact with Dyslexic kids. I want to give educators a better understanding of who we are and how we learn. My intention is to provide teachers with a more accurate and realistic view into the world of Dyslexia by offering them tools and strategies to help create a more positive learning experience for their Dyslexic students. My hope is that I can bring awareness about Dyslexia so that both the student and teacher can have a successful year together by removing some of the frustrations that may arise.

Following are a few easy suggestions for teachers to use in their classroom settings to help Dyslexic students succeed along with the rest of their students:

Keep the following words and ideas in mind when you come across a Dyslexic kid, as it will forever change your success rate as a teacher in a very positive and rewarding way. Guaranteed!

- When you know a Dyslexic child is in your class, **please write down the homework assignments on the board**, and keep instructions simple.
- If you give the assignments/instructions verbally, do remember to give one instruction at a time, and make sure to double-check with your student to make sure he understood and wrote all the assignments down in his homework journal.
- Another simple suggestion is to write assignments on the board FIRST THING when you come in the morning so students can get a real chance to transcribe the assignment in their homework journal during the day. They cannot always fully comprehend or retain all the information when it is given only verbally, but when they can see the words written on the board and hear them verbally, they have a much higher rate of success.
- Nowadays, the Internet is an amazing tool for Dyslexics. Assignments sent via e-mail help tremendously. This way, the instructions are clearly written, and it also eliminates the step of having to copy the assignment from the board. This is a tremendous help for Dyslexics, as it eliminates the chance of transcribing errors. And as a teacher, you will also be happy to see your students bring back their assignments completed on time and accurately.

Even today as an adult, I notice that when I take a class and get instructions by certain teachers, I still struggle to keep up or understand the instructions. It usually happens when the teacher uses very technical and wordy vocabulary and gives me numerous instructions to do at once.

To me, it feels like the teacher is speaking at the speed of light, and I end up completely disoriented. I find it super difficult to write what is on the board while the teacher is talking, as I'm focusing on remembering one thing and not the other. When the teacher is going too fast for me, I can't even think straight. Then I have to put myself in an awkward situation, as I have to ask the teacher to repeat the question again for me or ask the person next to me. This can be really embarrassing and discouraging for a Dyslexic person. Sometimes I feel bombarded by words being shot at me at one hundred miles per hour, and all it manages to do is just shut me down.

By just taking a few minutes to write the assignment down, you can help us succeed, and as a teacher, isn't that your goal anyway? Remember, we need visuals! So write it on the board early in the morning, write it on a paper for us, or even e-mail it to us, and you will help us; and at the same time, you'll also be less stressed too. It's a win-win situation.

Since one out of five students may have learning difficulties, isn't it worth removing as many frustrations and stressors as possible so both the teacher and the student can succeed?

Even though there's been great progress made in the field of Dyslexia in America, most public schools remain traditionally set up by and for left-brain thinkers. And since, as Dyslexics, we typically learn and navigate the world differently, school remains a daily challenge for us. I understand that making changes to the school curriculum could be hard work and costly to the school system, but I also think that there are so many of us who are going through this system today that accommodations need to be implemented if we truly want the system to work. Most importantly, by making even just a few changes to the curriculum, left-brain thinkers will continue to understand and succeed, but now we will also have the right-brain thinkers increase their chances of success.

I understand that typical public school systems are based on speed, but honestly, in the grand scheme of things, it's not that important in real life. Learning to read, write, and do math is important, but the fact that it takes me a few minutes more to answer a math fact quiz won't determine my success ratio in the real world. Those kinds of tests are a sure way to crush a Dyslexic child's self-esteem, self-confidence, and it ends up actually hurting him in the long run. I would love to see a change in the school system, and at the same time, I'm very realistic and see it's going to take a long time to turn the system around and make significant changes to the structure. And in the meantime, we Dyslexics will continue to work twice as hard and will persevere.

Teachers, if you suspect that one of your students may be Dyslexic, please, at least, let the parents know so they can help their child. I can understand you are overwhelmed and stressed by your workload and student-teacher ratio, but as a teacher, you aspire to help every single child in your class succeed. You may not have the training necessary to help per se, but you can at least direct the child to someone who can help, and the sooner the better. Every day a child is left unlabeled is one more day when his self-esteem is put in danger.

Through my years of research on Dyslexia, I have read numerous times that in public schools, teachers may not always have the resources needed to help, even though they may recognize that one or two kids in their class may be Dyslexic. Because some teachers are so overwhelmed with the number of students in the class, the disruptive kids, and the many other circumstances going on in the classroom on a daily basis, the Dyslexic kids get kind of forgotten. This usually happens because Dyslexic kids tend to be quiet and nondisruptive, as they are trying really hard to minimize their chances of being put on the spot, knowing they may not be able to answer a question or they may be asked to read aloud in front of the class. These kids feel embarrassed, so they tend to remain quiet.

In my opinion, having more parents recognize the signs of Dyslexia as soon as possible and become advocates for their kids will increase their children's chances of success. So, teachers, please let parents know as soon as possible if you suspect a student may be Dyslexic. This way, the parent can seek help right away. Parents can then pursue alternative and supplementary help outside the traditional school setting, in addition to the help you give them.

If you are a teacher reading this book, please take the following advice seriously and bring it back with you to your classroom. Just think how you can help a child succeed and empower him for life by remembering the following:

- Be patient with us. We are not stupid; we just learn differently.
- Be understanding. We are not lazy. We just use much more energy to write than others. We are doing the best we can at that moment.
- Give us positive reinforcement, not negative reinforcement. We need encouragement and praise for our efforts, as we are trying much harder than other students, even if it's not always obvious at first sight.
- We can DO and learn anything we put our minds to. We just need time on our side.
- Be tolerant and understanding with us, and you'll be amazed by what we achieve.
- When you think we are uncooperative, not trying hard enough, unfocused, not listening . . . stop and *look* at us! Think, "What can I do to help this student at this moment?"
  - Give a positive or kind word.
  - Offer more time to complete an assignment.
  - Show more patience and compassion.
  - Give another example (be **more concrete**).
- When you see that we are disorganized, don't yell at us and embarrass us in front of our friends. Instead, help us find a

system and solution. Give us ideas and suggestions; that's all we need and want.

Even as an adult, I'm challenged by the simple act of writing. I can write much easier and for longer periods of time when I use a keyboard (even with no formal keyboard training). So, teachers, when you think we are being lazy, we may in fact be exhausted. Schools need to let Dyslexic students use computers more frequently.

Some teachers understand us, and they are **fantastic**. Those kinds of teachers make school so enjoyable! We've had the good fortune to have many of these great teachers, and they are a true blessing and a gift!

My final thought for teachers is this: Take the time to listen and understand your Dyslexic students a little better. They have a lot to offer this world and are eager to contribute when given an opportunity.

A Dyslexic's ability to think in 3-D, his passionate and imaginative creativity, and his wealth of knowledge will blow you away. My son's teachers are always amazed and impressed by FéZander's depth of knowledge and the insights he brings to the classroom.

"Dear Teachers" in Summary for the Right-Brain Thinker and Dyslexic

I think that this part of my book is very important and every word matters, which makes it very difficult for me to summarize this section. So in keeping the Dyslexics' reading difficulties in mind, along with wanting every single word of this chapter to be captured, I decided to do a video on my website of this entire chapter.

In this video, I, along with Doug's help, will personally read to you the entire chapter of "Dear Teachers." And by now you know, reading aloud is a HUGE challenge for ME, but I feel you deserve to hear this part of the book in full. Now you see why I'm UN-Stoppable! I take risks and challenge myself every day! Hope you enjoy!

***Please go to our website:
www.DyslexicAndUnstoppable.com
Click on:
"Dear Teachers" video

PART 3

Tools and Strategies

I n this section, we will provide you with tools and strategies that actually work or have worked for us. Some tools we still use, and some we don't need anymore. The ideas listed below are strategies that benefited our son. After many years of research and numerous trials and errors, the following are what worked best in our case. Even though every Dyslexic has his own individual challenges and degree of difficulties, there are common signs and symptoms associated with Dyslexia. So hopefully our suggestions will help you and your child. Basically, you take the ideas that work for you, and you let go of the rest.

Again, we can speak only from OUR own experience. These tips were practical, concrete, and easy for us to navigate. Some are daily practices we do, advice we received, and simple solutions that work for us. In the end, we hope they will help you too!

We are very excited about this section, as we put a lot of effort and love in the design and structure of this chapter. We built this section of the book specifically with Dyslexics in mind, for the young ones as much as the adult ones. Our model is based on visual aids and simple explanations to help the Dyslexic person understand the concepts clearly and easily.

The following tools and strategies are accompanied by instructional videos on our website DyslexicAndUNStoppable.com. Basically, we will enumerate the tools or strategies in the book and explain the process in videos on our website. Very cool, right? Each short video will be titled and named the same as the tool or strategy in this chapter.

Since I'm Dyslexic and the one writing this book, I figured that I can design it any way that pleases me. So therein lie the video instructions. A Dyslexic helping Dyslexics! And most importantly, since half of the time I don't understand the instructions on paper, I figured that as a Dyslexic or parent of one, you would also benefit from the videos as much as I do. Videos and audiobooks have changed the lives of thousands and thousands of Dyslexics, so we will do the same process with our book and revolutionize the book industry in favor of Dyslexics! More power to US as we are UN-Stoppable!

Many of these tools were learned from other teachers. We have adapted them to make them more practical in our lives. Wherever possible, we have given credit in the video to the original source.

The Alphabet Test (Video)

See "The Alphabet Test" video on our website.

- We will do a demonstration with a Dyslexic child and a non-Dyslexic child and show you both results for comparison.
- Dr. Curtiss will explain the exercise and the results on the video.

Pencils and Tools (Video)

See "Pencils and Tools" video on our website.

- We use triangular-shaped pencils instead of regular circular-shaped ones. These pencils help us have a better grip and get less tired from writing.
- I use pencils more than pen. This way I can erase easily and start over if I need to rewrite a word. Obviously, computers are the best for this, but it is not realistic to think I can write all my work, tasks, and ideas on the computer. So I need to be able to write.

Helpful Supplements (Video)

See "Helpful Supplements" video on our website.

- Homeopathic products for focus, concentration, nausea (inner ear—more details in video)
- Fish oils
- Fatty acids

Food and Nutrition (Video)

See "Food and Nutrition" video on our website.

- Diet:
  - Fresh fruits
  - Vegetables
  - Salmon, fish, canned tuna
  - Protein
  - Ground flaxseeds, flaxseed oil
  - Wheat germ
- *READ labels! We stay away as much as possible from:
  - Fast food
  - Processed food
  - Food dyes
  - Food preservatives
  - Food additives

- We replaced white sugar in recipes with pure maple sugar, pure maple syrup, and organic coconut sugar.
- Water: We drink filtered water as much as possible.
- Sodas: Only on special occasions and usually without caffeine, like root beer.
- Juices: We only occasionally drink fruit juices, and we buy organic when available.

Speech (Video)

See "Speech" video on our website.
- See a professional speech therapist as early as possible.
- Many easy and useful exercises are free online.
- "Speech buddies" to do @ home (We bought online.)

Skin and Allergies (Video)

See "Skin and Allergies" video on our website.
- Recurrent allergies and ear/sinus infections and the correlation with Dyslexia.
- (Prevention is the best medicine. This topic will be discussed in more detail by Dr. Curtiss in the video.)

Fine Motor Help and Accommodations (Video)

See "Fine Motor Help and Accommodations" video on our website.
- Computer (learn typing skills; many free online websites)
- Finally, we get a break in school. With the new emphasis put on technologies in school and since technology is now becoming a daily part of the school requirements, we finally have turned the tide. Now the odds are in our favor because we have this visual gift and usually do better with technology.

- The introduction of technologies in the schools has drastically improved our odds of succeeding in the traditional schools and makes our school years more pleasant and enjoyable.
- Dr. Curtiss will explain in more detail tools like:
  - Dragon Dictation®
  - SmartPens®
  - Voice messaging on phones

This minimizes duplicate writing and errors, thus making writing time more enjoyable and less time-consuming.

- Clothing and shoes: You know the saying: "Pick your battles." Well, here we work with what we have and disregard the rest. Keep it simple!
- Limit your energy waste and frustrations by focusing on the positive.
  - Shoes
  - Clothing
  - Pants
  - Tops
- All the tricks that we have learned to make dressing easier will be discussed on the video.

Math (Video)
See "Math" video on our website.

- Math cards: We will do a demonstration in our math video. You can also go to DianeCraft.org for more detailed information.
- Use graph paper: Dr. Curtiss will explain in more detail in the video the reason we use graph paper. It has to do with the alignment of the numbers in a math problem. Ninety percent of

errors in my son's math problems are based on alignment issues instead of calculation errors. He understands the problem quite well but sometimes misaligns the numbers, which in turn can give him the wrong answer. Now that he is aware of this, he pays greater attention to the alignment in his math problems, and the results show.

Spelling (Video)

See "Spelling" video on our website.

Dr. Curtiss will explain in greater detail (in the videos), the difference between the left-brain thinkers and the right-brain thinkers when it comes to learning spelling words and sight words.

For example, the left-brain thinkers learn by repeating and writing the words over and over, but for the Dyslexics, this method is useless. In my experience, I found this to be one of the most challenging concepts to discuss with left-brain thinkers. Getting them to accept and understand this concept is sometimes impossible. They strongly believe that their method of learning is the right way. This traditional programming of repetition is so deeply ingrained in our society that it makes it very difficult to change people's way of thinking, even when it's in the best interest of the child.

During the school year, FéZander usually has a spelling test weekly.

Usually on Mondays, the teachers give the students a pretest on about ten to twenty words. My son's scores are quite variable on the pretests, depending on the complexity of the words. That evening, he brings home his spelling words list, and that's when the work begins. First, we find the common denominators, and then we divide the words. In general, we practice the words every day until the testing day. And in most cases, he usually does very well on the tests. The key points for my son are daily practice and being able to form a mental picture of the word in his head. Practicing a little every day instead of all the words at the last minute is also very important and makes a huge difference when the test day comes around.

The association of the word with the picture is crucial. One easy example is with the sound "OW." On an index card, draw a picture of a cow, and on the cow's belly write the letters OW. This helps the Dyslexic child make the connection between the two sides of his brain. And when the Dyslexic child can see it, then he can remember it forever!

Another example:

Un/comfort/able

Divide the word and use different colors. No cost to you and can easily be done at home. More examples will be provided in the video.

Dyslexics work so much harder physically and mentally than the so-called normal kids at understanding certain concepts, but when they get it, THEY GET IT!

When it is clear and visual in their heads (minds), they never forget it because they can always go retrieve and access that picture and do it again and again.

Sight Words

These are words that can't be sounded out and to which grammar rules don't apply. You basically just need to learn them, and that's that. Since they follow their own grammar rules, you can see how difficult these words can be for Dyslexics to learn. They make no sense and cannot be associated with something concrete UNTIL we start learning them the right-brain way. Again here, draw a picture on a flash card that your child associates with this word and write the word on the picture.

Examples will be shown in videos of:

- Black-and-white sight words cards versus color-coded cards
- Cards that show the sound with a picture

One thing we were able to do, which may be useful for your child, was to ask the schoolteacher for the sight-word list for the coming year. With the list in hand, we made flash cards with the pictures and practiced during the summer before school started. A little practice four or five days a week makes a big difference. Only do five to ten minutes per day or five words or so per day so that there's a time limit.

My kid performs and works so much more efficiently when we do things like:

Two pages of spelling per day or twenty words of speech or ten minutes of reading. You need to be specific and stick to that rule and give lots and lots of positive reinforcements. My kid loves *Legos*, science, and history. So he saves his reward money for special buys. He has a reward chart where he accumulates stickers (they have different values for different tasks). Being Dyslexic is a full-time job for a kid. So we feel our son deserves to be rewarded for his hard work and determination. What a gift he's giving to himself.

Figure 8 (Video)

See "Figure 8" (our interpretation) video on our website.

For more details and explanation, visit the author's website, www. DianeCraft.org.

Organization

We use lots of plastic colored dividers and folders to organize and divide the different school subjects (math, science, language arts, social studies, etc.). You can buy them at your local office supply store. We usually buy plastic and sturdy folders, as they are more cost efficient. They last longer and cost you less money in the long run. We systematize our binders and make it as simple as possible for FéZander to remember. One folder is for the homeroom teacher assignments and materials, and the other for the so-called *specials* (for example, Latin, science, social studies).

Where's my stuff? It disappeared again!

My advice: label everything, buy in bulk, and chill out! My son leaves a trail all around the school campus (like squirrels leave their nuts for the winter). One glove over here, one over there. My trumpet over here and my snack bag over there. Thankfully, we have super nice and understanding teachers and a great school principal. One day you can see the principal walking around with FéZander's trumpet and bringing his books back to the library. On another day, five lunch bags are coming back home in FéZander's backpack. But most importantly, everyone loves and accepts my son just the way he is, and that's awesome. They see his kindness, smartness, and eagerness to learn, and put aside the rest. Now that's not something you see every day! Associate with people who see the best in you and you will succeed in life!

You know the saying "pick your battles"? Well, here we work with what we have and simplify the rest.

Snack/lunch: brown bag and recyclables. If your kid can't remember to bring the lunch bag home every day and you do not want him or you stressed about it, then have him eat a hot lunch or use brown bags. (Eat, put the bag in the trash and the water bottle in the recycle bin, and be done.)

Reading Classes

See "Reading Classes" video on our website.

Choosing the right reading classes makes all the difference for Dyslexics.

By being in the right remedial reading classes, my son went from kindergarten level to second grade level in two months. And by the end of fourth grade, FéZander had a tenth-grade comprehension level. Today he's an avid reader (AKA "bookworm"). It's such a beautiful thing to see!

As we know, every Dyslexic child is different, with varying degrees of difficulties. So this may mean that for some children, their reading difficulties may linger and remain unresolved.

In the end, if reading ends up being your least strong suit, so what? Find your path, your strengths, and what makes you passionate and do that! We all have different jobs we need to do in this world, so you might as well figure out early what you are great at and follow that dream. All you can do is try your best and go with your passion.

In the Dyslexia community, it is suggested to start remedial reading lessons as soon as possible to alleviate the chances of your child becoming discouraged. The sooner you start, the better he will do.

The use of colored gels or colored plastic film when reading books helped FéZander, as the words on pages didn't move as much. The gels changed the way the light reflected on the pages, thus removing the glare. If I remember correctly, green ones worked best for my son.

We will do a demonstration in our video. (Visit the product section of our website to purchase these colored gels.)

A newer product on the market is called "colored reading glasses." It is supposed to have promising results. Since these were not available when we first started remedial reading classes, we never had the opportunity to try them. I would suggest asking your reading teacher or checking the web for more details. We just wanted to let you know these are available and may be helpful for your child.

Reading options in school: If we were given the option of learning with audiobooks in school, there would be many more successful Dyslexics in traditional schools. Ask your school; maybe you will get lucky!

When available or possible, keep a textbook at home and one at school.

We listen to audiobooks in the car and at bedtime. At my house, we all go to bed early so we can read before falling asleep. We started this habit at a very young age with our kids, and now they look forward to this relaxing time. It's a great habit, and FéZander really enjoys it. He was able to accumulate hours of reading time in a fun and positive way.

Reading aloud is a very important practice for Dyslexics. This helps them engage both sides of their brain simultaneously. For Dyslexics, reading aloud is very laborious.

So be patient with your child and find ways to make it as fun and positive as possible, as it can be very stressful for your child. Acknowledging your child's effort and being supportive will help diminish his anxiety and make him feel understood, thus increasing his chances of success.

The following are great ways to work both sides of your brain:

- Learning to play an instrument (one can learn online or from library books and CDs). Private lessons worked best for us, as we could go at our own speed and enjoy the process at the same time without the pressure of keeping up with the other students.
- Learn a second language as young as possible. It is scientifically proven that learning a second language as young as possible makes you "smarter." Put in simple terms, it helps your brain retain and engage your neurons. There are countless ways to learn a second language. For us, because I'm French, we took private lessons because, where we live, French is not offered in the public schools. We have friends who took a second language at the school and others who took advantage of the local library's resources. We also know people who bought a computer program and others who took classes online. So you can see there are countless ways of learning a second language. The method you choose is only a preference. What's important is learning the second language as young as possible.
- Learn to play chess. We were lucky, since parents from our local elementary school organized after-school chess classes a few times per year. We also knew friends who took lessons at the

local library. Again, chess is just another great way of engaging both sides of your brain and learning critical thinking strategies. Personally, I was never interested in learning to play chess. But to my surprise, both my kids enjoy playing chess. So even though you as a parent may not be inspired to play chess, your child might be. Just keep it in mind if the opportunity shows up around you.

- Learn martial arts. I have a deep connection with martial arts. I did judo when I was young, and as an adult, I've been practicing tae kwon do two or three times every week for the past four years. It keeps me grounded and helps me alleviate the daily stresses from my body and mind. Learning *forms* helps me focus and concentrate better by learning and practicing patterns. It helps with coordination, sequences, memorization, and constantly working on remembering left and right. And it's a great positive environment for socializing with like-minded people. It is quite humbling to learn tae kwon do, as you need constant perseverance, integrity, courage, and lots and lots of patience. Martial arts are often offered at your local recreational center, library, or YMCA, just to name a few.

- Swimming lessons. Over the years, we learned that wearing swim goggles helped diminish the reflection on the water so that my son becomes less disoriented during swim lessons. He can perform and learn faster with the swim goggles. When my son doesn't wear his goggles in the pool while doing long laps, he has more difficulty keeping oriented and finding where he is heading in the pool.

- One-on-one instruction. We often find that one-on-one classes and instruction work better for us than some group lessons. During swimming lessons and music, for example, private classes accelerate the learning process, as we get better and faster results. This way, the teacher has more time to work with us and is more patient with our needs. When you are in a group lesson, often the teacher needs to stick to the schedule and keep going, even when some kids do not completely understand the task at hand for that day. This way, a child can easily fall behind and get lost. Other times it's good and productive to follow the group, as you get this extra push to get going with the "group energy." It just depends on the goal and the nature of the class. When FéZander takes a class for pure enjoyment or just for fun, then we do not do private lessons and all is well, since part of the class is for socialization, like tennis, chess, art, and woodworking.

"Tools and Strategies" in Summary for the Right-Brain Thinker and Dyslexic

Basically, the summary for this chapter, "Tools and Strategies," is available in the video portion of our website. This is purposely designed to help Dyslexics understand and absorb the wealth of information gathered in this book. Visit our website at www.DyslexicAndUNStoppable.com to view our extensive collection of videos.

I would like to remind all the left-brain parents and teachers that this way of thinking is different from what you are accustomed to, but will still work for you. And most importantly, this book is to help your Dyslexic child or student. Your preferences in learning will need to be put aside for the time being. These learning techniques and strategies are designed to help your child succeed. So take the time to do it, and see the positive changes happen. You will surely be amazed!

Being Dyslexic myself, I totally see it and understand this way of learning because I'm also part of this right-brain thinking world. So this way of learning is very rewarding and engaging for me. But then I have my husband, the Ivy League graduate and total left-brain thinker, who learns totally differently. He wants facts, black-and-white books, and in-depth explanations.

Doug, as a father and as a husband, is able to put his learning preferences aside to help our son with his homework and me with my tae kwon do *forms*.

FéZander uses right-brain thinking strategies and tools all the time, and the results are apparent and consistent. In my view, results are milestones to show us the progress he has made, and we certainly see progress. We see progress in every aspect of our son's life: school, sports, social interactions, creativity and so on. This is really just the beginning for him. Today, FéZander is truly UN-Stoppable!

To take advantage of all of the extras, including supplemental videos, visit:

www.DyslexicAndUnstoppable.com
Click on: Book Extras
Enter the password: Unstoppable

PART 4

Dyslexic and UN-Stoppable:
A Pediatrician's and
Dad's Perspective

By now you have probably noticed that this is not a normal book about Dyslexia. (Besides, what Dyslexic person wants to be "normal"?) You have probably noticed that this book does not go on and on with endless facts about Dyslexia or talk about the limitations Dyslexia places on your life. This book is all about practical solutions to help your Dyslexic child excel in life. Sprinkled in between these suggestions is our story of how we overcame Dyslexia and used it to make the life of our dreams. Now comes the pediatrician's chapter. Maybe you are concerned that there will be lots of medical terms and difficult-to-understand messages filled with jargon. Don't worry. This chapter will be just like the rest of the book, clear and concise and easy to read. Yes, I have to confess. I am not a Dyslexic, and I am a left-brain thinker. Still, we'll make this chapter as much fun as the rest. It will be mostly in question-and-answer form, with specific actions that you can take to help your child with Dyslexia become UN-Stoppable.

Many of these questions are from actual parents who have come into my office over the past fifteen years of my pediatric practice. So let's get started.

Questions About Dyslexia

What is Dyslexia?

So what is Dyslexia anyway? A quick search of the web will find many definitions of Dyslexia, some of which we mentioned in the first chapter. It can be described as:

"Difficulties in acquiring and processing language that is typically manifested by a lack of proficiency in reading and writing" (www. merriamwebster.com).

And

"Brain-based type of learning disability that specifically impairs a person's ability to read . . . difficulty with spelling, phonological processing (the manipulation of sound) and/or rapid visual-verbal responding" (The National Institute of Neurological Disorders and Stroke).

To the average person, these definitions may not be helpful. Most people hear "Dyslexia" and think that it is all about reading backwards. Yet, while letter reversals can happen with Dyslexia, there is so much more involved. So let's break it down. Basically, Dyslexia is characterized by a difficulty in breaking words into their "sound parts" that allow you to sound out the word. In our own life, this showed up when our son, FéZander, transitioned from having to read the so-called sight words to reading sentences. When learning the sight words, there was no requirement to sound the word out. He was shown a word and told to memorize what it was.

Since he, like so many Dyslexics, is brilliant, this memorization was easy. However, when he was exposed to other words that he had to sound out, that is when the Dyslexia revealed itself.

How does one get Dyslexia?

Generally speaking, Dyslexia is thought to be genetic. This means that it tends to run in families. However, just because a parent has Dyslexia, does not mean that his or her child will absolutely have Dyslexia. The genetics are more complex than that, and there are probably other factors that influence it. Most likely, Dyslexia arises when the brain is developing and the nerve cells move and connect with each other in a certain way that is different from the average person. Because the process is so involved, the genetics may not be obvious. In our own family, we did not recognize the genetics until our son was diagnosed. Then we were able to trace Dyslexia back to his mother (the author of this book) and probably several other relatives.

How common is Dyslexia?

It is estimated that Dyslexia occurs in approximately 15–20 percent of the population. Of course, Dyslexia is not an all-or-none phenomenon. People can have varying degrees of Dyslexia, with some people having only mild difficulties in reading and others more severely affected. However, at 15–20 percent of the population, Dyslexia is more common than blue eyes and left-handedness.

In my view, since Dyslexia is so common, we need to stop thinking about Dyslexia as a disorder and start thinking about it as a difference in learning that requires a different approach in teaching.

Are there any specific groups of people that are more affected by Dyslexia?

Dyslexia seems to be spread across the population equally. There is no difference in the frequency of Dyslexia between males and females or different ethnic groups or socioeconomic classes. Lower socioeconomic status may be associated with more severe Dyslexia, but this is probably related to a disparity in services that they can afford to provide to their kids. In any society with reading and written language, there are people with Dyslexia.

I have a child with Dyslexia, and now I am expecting my second child. What are the chances that the baby will be born with Dyslexia too?

Because the genetics are not exactly defined and are very complex, it is difficult to predict the inheritance of Dyslexia. Researchers have found certain genes associated with Dyslexia. However, there are most likely multiple genes involved, and of course, environmental factors play a role. Current estimates are that if one sibling has Dyslexia, there is a 30–60 percent chance that other siblings are affected. The important thing is to have a high index of suspicion.

So when the new baby begins to talk and then to read, pay close attention to see if he has the same issues as the older sibling. That way, you can start reading interventions right away.

I want to be sure to recognize Dyslexia early. What are some early signs that my child has Dyslexia?

Children with Dyslexia may have issues with language development that show up as speaking later than their non-Dyslexic counterparts. They may show difficulty learning new words and may even have trouble rhyming words. They may memorize the sight words, but interchange one for another. Since one of the first words children learn to spell is often their own names, an early clue to Dyslexia may be a child's inability to recognize the letters of his own name. Since FéZander's actual name is Félix-Alexander, we always thought that his difficulty in spelling it was due to having such a long name. It was later, when we discovered that he was Dyslexic, that we figured out the real reason. It was his Dyslexia all along. If you see these clues in your child, pay close attention to his reading development and get him help as soon as you see problems.

I'm pretty sure my child has Dyslexia. What should I do next?

When parents suspect that their child may have Dyslexia, the most important thing is to get the child help as soon as possible.

Studies have shown that the earlier a child with Dyslexia receives help, the better the outcome is. The first step parents should take is to determine if they want to pursue help through the school system, through private avenues, or both. For many parents, there is the concern about labeling a child.

However, if Dyslexia is presented to the child as simply a different way of learning, with its strengths and challenges, a way of learning that just requires a different way of teaching, the child will accept it as part of his life and move on.

I plan to have my child tested in the school system (after all, that is why I pay taxes). What should I expect?

If you do decide to go through the school system, make sure you familiarize yourself with the laws in your state and school system. As stated below, the Individuals with Disabilities Education Act requires that schools provide free education to all students regardless of any disability. However, whether or not a child qualifies for special education services depends on how the disability is affecting his schooling. For example, it may be difficult to obtain services for a Dyslexic child who is performing at grade level. Your pediatrician can help you to figure out this complicated system and write letters to the school system for you that help your child get the services he needs.

What are the steps involved in having my child evaluated by the school?

The first step is for you to request that your child be evaluated for special education services. This request should be in writing and addressed to the school board.

The school system then has sixty days to make a determination as to whether the child is eligible for services. If the child is determined to be eligible, the school system must schedule an Individualized Education Program meeting to develop an IEP as well as a plan for implementation. As you can see, this process can take ninety days. So you want to be in continual contact with the school system to move things along.

I don't want to involve the school. Where can I turn to get services?

There are many resources for Dyslexia, both in your local area and online. When searching for services, it is best to search for services related to a specific challenge that your child is having rather than generic Dyslexia services. To find testing and tutoring centers in your area, the following resources can help:

As far as online services, here are a few by category:

Reading

www.orton-gillingham.us

This site is developed by the Institute for Multi-Sensory Instruction. It contains resources such as educational apps categorized by school year. Lower elementary apps include ABC Phonics, Site Words, Phonics Tic Tac Toe, and Cimo Spelling Site. Upper elementary school apps include spelling apps and grammar apps. There are even apps for vocabulary, as well as Latin and Greek roots for middle and high school students.

www.interdys.org

This is the website for the International Dyslexia Association and contains a bookstore with workbooks and textbooks for parents of kids with Dyslexia.

Spelling

www.spellzone.com

This is a site that has games and activities to enhance spelling and make it fun to learn.

www.beatingDyslexia.com/spellinghelp.html

Offers tricks to help learn spelling words.

Math

www.learningresources.com

Purchase items such as Cuisenaire rods, which offer a hands-on method to learn math facts.

www.mathusee.com

Allows you to generate worksheets to practice math.

Organization Skills

www.Dyslexia.yale.edu/DYS_Student2Student.html

Contains tips from Dyslexic students to help overcome any Dyslexia challenge, including organizational difficulties.

Dysgraphia

www.dianecraft.org

Offers tools and exercises to improve dysgraphia, a commonly associated difficulty.

http://www.ncld.org/students-disabilities/assistive-technology-education/apps-students-ld-dysgraphia-writing-difficulties

Has assistive tools for kids with dysgraphia.

My son is in fourth grade and was just identified with Dyslexia. Is it too late to help him?

It is never too late to help your child with Dyslexia. While it is true that early intervention helps improve outcomes, any help that you can give your child will make a difference. Lucie, the author of this book, is an excellent example of this. She did not discover her Dyslexia until her twenties. Yet she is now running a company and writing a book. Besides, kids are so intuitively smart that your son has probably found ways of compensating for the Dyslexia without even knowing it. Now that you know what is going on, you can help him even more.

What are some other disorders or difficulties associated with Dyslexia?

There are some disorders that people with Dyslexia are more predisposed to. These include:

- **Dysgraphia.** This is simply an impaired ability to write. It often shows up as difficulty with penmanship and becoming easily fatigued when required to write. These students often seem to hate to write, and answers to questions may seem short and incomplete. However, when allowed to type a story or recall it verbally, they are able to show their creativity and knowledge.
- **Dyscalculia.** This is an impairment in the ability to perform math functions that is not related to intelligence.
- **Left-right confusion.** Because Dyslexia may involve the communication of information from one side of the brain to the other, people with Dyslexia often confuse their left and right.

The goal of this section is not to have you focus on your child's weaknesses. Instead, by realizing what other issues are associated with

Dyslexia, you can recognize them early and get your child the necessary help to improve them.

How does Dyslexia affect my son's ability to do math?

While Dyslexia is predominantly a reading and language disorder, it can affect other areas of a child's education, such as math. In particular, memorizing math facts can be difficult for a child with Dyslexia. They often understand complex math concepts, yet have trouble with retaining the basic math facts, such as multiplication tables. Rote memorization using flash cards is not the best approach for these kids. If the flash cards contain pictures, they may help. Other effective techniques include using physical objects to demonstrate math facts or allowing a student to draw out the math problem as a picture. When it comes to doing two-digit math, use graph paper to help your child line up the numbers appropriately.

How does Dyslexia affect spelling, and what can I do to help my child in this area?

Certainly, spelling is an area that can present a problem for kids with Dyslexia. The key to helping your child master spelling is to realize that Dyslexics do not respond well to rote memorization. Simply drilling and drilling the words over and over does not help a Dyslexic. It is better to find ways to incorporate as many parts of the child's brain into learning the spelling words. Use flash cards with the words written over a picture that describes each sound to incorporate the visual part of the brain. Have your child spell out loud to incorporate the auditory part of the brain. Use a small sandbox in which your child spells the word with his finger.

This brings in the tactile part of the brain. The key to spelling is to make it as multisensory as possible to incorporate the whole brain. This will improve the chances that the spelling words become permanent in your child's memory.

My child is starting seventh grade and needs to take a foreign language. How does Dyslexia affect one's ability to learn a foreign language?

Foreign languages can present a unique problem for kids with Dyslexia. As mentioned above, Dyslexic students have difficulty with what is called phonemic awareness, or how different combinations of letters create different sounds. This makes it difficult for them to sound out new words, even in English.

Foreign languages present a unique challenge.

Not only are there the same issues as in English, such as reading and sounding out words and spelling, but also foreign languages have their own unique phonemes. Letter combinations that produce one sound in English may produce a totally different sound in another language.

Thankfully, there are effective techniques for Dyslexic students to learn a new language. For example, the researchers Ganschow and Spark found that by using the Orton-Gillingham techniques of incorporating visual, tactile (or touch), and kinesthetic (or movement) cues into foreign language learning, children with Dyslexia can master a foreign language.

If I decide to ask the school system for accommodations, what are some specific accommodations that I should ask for?

Accommodations that your child may need will be unique to your child, based on his specific challenges. The good news is that if you do decide to involve the school, they are obligated to assess your child's strengths and areas of concern and come up with a specific educational plan to help remediate, or at least accommodate, where there is a need.

According to the Individuals with Disabilities Education Act (IDEA), states are required to provide a "free, appropriate public education" in the "least restrictive environment."

Accommodations that frequently make a big impact for kids with Dyslexia include:

- Systems to help with copying homework assignments off the blackboard.
- Asking the teacher to simply glance at the student's assignment book and ensure that all assignments are included.
- Using e-mail to send assignments directly home.
- Using printed sheets rather than requiring the child to copy the assignments.
- Having two sets of textbooks, one for home and one for school.
- Using electronic reminders, such as an alarm on a cell phone (if allowed) to remind the student to bring all homework home.
- Institute routines so that the student has a checklist of things to remember before coming home (e.g., double-check board for assignments, check that he has all books in his book bag, etc.).
- Oral, rather than written, instructions for tests.
- Oral testing altogether. Since the purpose of testing is to assess a student's knowledge on a given subject, the student should be given every chance to prove what he knows, including using methods other than written tests.

The school system is questioning ADHD, but I think there is something more than that going on. What should I do?

Whenever a child is fidgeting in his seat or appears not to be paying attention, it can be tempting to think of attention deficit hyperactive disorder as the reason. After all, this can be easily treated with medication.

However, many other disorders can give the impression of attention problems, including Dyslexia.

In our own lives, before we figured out that our son had Dyslexia, we even considered ADHD. Why? Often, when it was time for FéZander to read (or worse, write) something for school, he would become antsy. He would begin to wiggle in his chair, play with his pencil, start talking about something else, or just get out of his chair. It would be easy to blame this on his attention. However, when the project was something he enjoyed, like building Legos, designing a machine, or even listening to stories, his attention was amazing. As soon as we enrolled him in the classes for Dyslexia and that was no longer a problem, his supposed attention problem went away.

If you find yourself in a similar situation, remember the following:

- Stick to your guns. You don't need to be belligerent with the school, but you do need to have your opinions heard.
- Remember, they may be the experts, but you know your child best.
- Insist on a planning and placement team to evaluate your child and come up with a plan.
- Ask your pediatrician to write a letter advocating testing for Dyslexia.
- If need be, obtain a referral from your pediatrician for private testing and evaluation that you can then bring to the school.

Eye tracking and Dyslexia

If you search online, you will discover plenty of sites that recommend various eye-tracking exercises to help improve a Dyslexic child's reading. These sites argue that the reading difficulty that occurs with Dyslexia happens because the child's eyes have difficulty tracking from left to right along a line of words. Therefore, they advocate exercises to improve the eyes' ability to focus and track the words on the page. But do these exercises actually do anything?

The effectiveness of visual tracking exercises in the treatment of Dyslexia is quite controversial. Unfortunately, most controlled studies have not demonstrated an improvement in reading with these exercises. This is probably because there are multiple brain systems involved in reading, not just the visual system. Since phonics-based systems using a multisensory approach have been shown to be most effective, it probably makes more sense to put one's time and energy into these proven forms of instruction.

Colored sheets and Dyslexia

Another popular aid for kids with Dyslexia is transparent sheets of different colors to lay over the page. These sheets purportedly also help improve the eye's tracking. Again, the efficacy of these sheets is unclear.

A study in the journal *Pediatrics* ("Irlen Colored Overlays Do not Alleviate Reading Difficulties," *Pediatrics*, 2011 Oct; 128(4):e9328. doi: 10.1542/peds.20110314.) did not find a benefit in reading speed and accuracy when using these sheets with children with Dyslexia. The study, however, only looked at sixty-one students in one class, so it is difficult to generalize the findings to all children.

Again, if parents decide to use these sheets, they simply need to be aware that their effectiveness is questionable. Some parents may feel that it cannot hurt to try.

As long as they do not take away from methods that are known to work, such as phonics-based, multisensory instruction, there is probably nothing wrong with trying them. Anecdotally, FéZander definitely seemed to benefit from them and would seek them out when he read at night.

Do brain exercises work?

If a person with Dyslexia has specific difficulties in decoding words and sounding out letter blends, can one exercise those parts of the brain that perform these functions and therefore improve reading? There is evidence that these exercises do help. A study in *Restorative Neuroscience and Neurology* in 2007 actually showed a change in children's brain function after undergoing sound training via computer exercises. We have a list of exercises that worked for us on **www.DyslexicAndUnstoppable.com.**

Do nutritional supplements help Dyslexia?

There is some evidence that the omega 3 fatty acids found in fish may help kids with Dyslexia. Of course, parents always needs to consult their own physicians before starting a supplement, but given all of the positive effects of omega 3 fatty acids on brain and heart health, they may definitely be an option for you.

Will someone with Dyslexia always have problems?

Can all the difficulties of Dyslexia be improved, or are there some limitations that a person with Dyslexia will always have? This often depends on a given student and his specific strengths and weaknesses. For example, with proper multisensory teaching techniques, most Dyslexic people will find that they can read proficiently. Any remaining weaknesses, such as spelling, can be overcome by appropriate assistive devices. For spelling, there is spell-check. For writing, there are typing and computers, or even dictation software. With all the amazing technology available, there really is no need to have any feature of Dyslexia stop your child from achieving an amazing life.

My child has Dyslexia. What profession should I encourage him to pursue?

There is no evidence that Dyslexic people are more or less successful in any given career than other people.

You can find people with Dyslexia in just about every profession known. Since a child's strengths and weaknesses are unique to that child, parents should cultivate their own child's strengths. Note what areas of school that your child enjoys most and seems to have an aptitude for, and then expose him to experiences that help him develop these areas.

"Dyslexic and UN-Stoppable: A Pediatrician's and Dad's Perspective" in Summary for the Right-Brain Thinker and Dyslexic

Rather than rehash this chapter in the summary, we have organized online videos with questions and answers, read by Dr. Curtiss.

Visit www.DyslexicAndUnstoppable.com for more information. Also stay tuned for webinars to get all your questions answered.

Epilogue

The best advice I can give you to help your child overcome Dyslexia is:

- Tell your teachers right away your child is or may be Dyslexic if you want the school to provide the appropriate services as soon as possible for your child.
- Start helping your child as early as you notice it. Don't wait until he's discouraged and feels like giving up.
- Be your child's best advocate and speak up for him. Teach the teachers and the community what works for your child, and remove those preconceived misconceptions from years ago. They did what they did at that time, as they did not know any better. Now we do know better and need to do better for our kids.
- Be extremely patient and understanding with your child.
- Join or form a community support group or master group.

- Like our Fan Page on Facebook to connect with other like-minded parents.
- Find a mentor/teacher your child loves, and nurture that friendship. It will propel your child into infinite possibilities. I did, and so did my son. (Thanks, Martin and Debra.)

It's wonderful when your parents believe in you, BUT it's life-changing when a mentor/teacher you respect believes in you. Sometimes mentors believe in you more than you do yourself at that moment, as they see your potential when it is hard for you to see it. My son once said to me: "M'man, I know you love me and believe I'm smart (as you tell me all the time) but when I heard it from another person, that's when I knew I was really smart! It's your job as a mom to remind me I can do it, but when I hear it from someone else, it's confirmation!" Words are so powerful. Use them wisely and do good.

Parents, I did my best to give you accurate and usable information, but remember, sometimes it will not make a significant difference, and your child may continue to struggle with reading, spelling, or math for the rest of his life. BUT, there's always hope! You have a brilliant child, and you need to find out what are his strengths and talents. What are your child's unique gifts and abilities? We all have special talents or gifts to share with the world; sometimes we just need a little time to figure them out. So, parents, give your kids wings and see them fly!

Spend time with your kids and make an extra effort to notice what really interests them.

Ask your kids questions about what they like, and let them try all kinds of different classes (art, science, sports). From there, see what makes them happy and what makes them want to go back to the class.

Which ones are they not as eager to go back to? What puts a smile on their faces? What makes them go back again and again? What makes their eyes sparkle? What motivates and nourishes their soul and their passion?

That's where you need to focus your energies and your child's energies. Nurture that part of your child and see him become UN-Stoppable! Those places and situations where your child succeeds, flourishes, and feels most happy and content are the answer!

Find the glitch in your kid and help him overcome it. Audiobooks are a fabulous tool for us, but they are not always available. So we need to have both options: reading with our eyes and with our ears. Your child may never be the best reader in the world, but as long as he's the best reader he can be, that's all that really matters.

One of the most important tasks for you as a parent is to find what your child likes and nurture it. It will change your child's life path in a positive and UN-Stoppable way!

Final Thoughts: Dyslexic—So What?

My Top Ten Accomplishments

(I can DO IT and so Can YOU)

Lucie

1. I won a bronze medal in judo in the Canada Winter Games.
2. I became a registered nurse.
3. I overcame six surgeries, two of which were major surgeries (complex molar pregnancy and fibroid).
4. I gave birth to my miracle child #1: FéZander.
5. I gave birth to my miracle child #2: Chloé.
6. I am an entrepreneur: I own and run a successful business.
7. I'm a fabulous mom (Maman, in my case).
8. I'm an adoring wife.

9. I'm a black belt in tae kwon do.
10. I Wrote THIS book!

(I can DO IT and so Can YOU)

FéZander

1. I'm a philanthropist.
2. I raised $610.25 to save the sharks and to bring awareness to their situation.
3. I created a website, www.WorldSharks.com.
4. I'm a great builder and innovative thinker (I've been making engineering books since I was four years old and inventing creative machines to make the world a better place and save the environment).
5. I'm a black belt in tae kwon do and do competitions.
6. I'm a top science kid.
7. I always win contests, like when I won my bike.
8. I rode in a helicopter.
9. I graduated from Tisko Elementary and was accepted at Hamden Hall.
10. I started taking personal development classes.

This is just to name a few. And we are just getting started. What ARE YOURS?

Acknowledgments

I have numerous people to thank and to whom I will forever be grateful for the love and support they have given to me, to FéZander, and to my family along this journey. These include the many **teachers** who helped FéZander during his schooling and went out of their way to give him extra attention and encouragement when it was needed. They also include **family** members who supported us when times seemed challenging.

Doug: Thank you to my PNM (Doug) for always having my back (no matter what!). You are willing to try new adventures with me, and by choosing to never settle for less than what you deserve, you give me the greatest gift of hope in our marriage. Our life together is always filled with fun challenges and amazing personal growth. Since you are such a fabulous pediatrician and enjoy being one, you could choose to coast. You could live the comfortable life, as you could easily do the same job for the rest of your career, since it's obvious that your patients/parents respect and trust you. Yet you choose to keep growing and expanding your comfort zone by trying new adventures with me. What a blessing you are, and I'm very grateful to be married to you!

My kids:

Chloé: Thank you, my "Cookie," for bringing joy into my life every day. Your awesome smile and laughter, your insightfulness, and your love of art are true gifts. Keep nurturing all those beautiful qualities in you, and believe in yourself; you are amazing! I'm so glad you are my girl!

Félix-Alexander: Thank you, FéZander, my "Baba"; your willingness to always try your best and determination are infectious. Your creativity and imagination (which are beyond words) and your compassionate heart are just a few of the blessings you bring us every day. I'm so honored to be your Maman. This world is so lucky to have you!

My dad (P'pa): I'm especially thankful for your willingness to recognize that as a parent the best gift you can give your child is the gift of CHOICE! By having the courage and strength to let me "fly with my own wings," you, in return, gave me the strength to face adversity and persevere no matter what. I know it's not easy to let go as a parent, but seeing your child fly on his own is worth it! I hope to do the same for my kids and let them be WHO THEY want to be! Now that's a truly courageous parent!

Martin: Thank you for seeing in me the potential that I didn't always see and kicking my b—t to achieve that potential. Now I know WHO I AM.

Debra: Thank you for seeing FéZander in all HIS brilliance and helping him see it also.

Extra: FéZander's Letter to Other Dyslexic Kids

Hello, I am Félix and I am Dyslexic. When my parents said I might be Dyslexic like Albert Einstein, I was begging to be Dyslexic. When my parents said I was Dyslexic, I was so happy. Then I went to a place so I could conquer the difficulties I had with Dyslexia. I now enjoy being Dyslexic and UN-Stoppable. There is nothing wrong with being Dyslexic. If you get the help you need, you can use the gift of Dyslexia you were given. I really like being Dyslexic, since I can do things others can't do. I know what it is like to be Dyslexic and know how hard it is if you don't go to a place for Dyslexics and you go to a school for non-Dyslexics.

FéZander with Master Han at our official black belt test on 12/15/2012

It won't help even if you do it 999,999,999,999 times. I also know that if you get the right help, you are UN-Stoppable. There is nothing wrong with Dyslexics or non-Dyslexics. They are just two ways of hooking up your brain. For non-Dyslexics, they learn both ways. Dyslexics learn a specific way. If you try to teach a non-Dyslexic child the Dyslexic way, they would understand, but if you try to teach a Dyslexic child the non-Dyslexic way, they wouldn't learn very well. Dyslexics are really creative, though, and that is one of the great things about Dyslexics. At first, my mom brought me to a place for kids who were falling behind in reading, but then I went to a place for Dyslexics, and I did more improving in the one for Dyslexics than non-Dyslexics. Now I study on things like poisonous snakes and how their venom works and how to cure it. I also learn about the weather's role in the defeat of Germany during WWII when they tried to take over Russia. You might not be interested in those things, but after you go to a place for Dyslexics, you will then be able to do whatever you want to do.

FéZander

About the Authors

Lucie M. Curtiss, RN

Lucie is a mother, nurse, entrepreneur, and the business manager of an extremely successful pediatric medical practice. Lucie is also Dyslexic. Having grown up in the French part of Canada in the 1970s, she did not even know that she was Dyslexic until adulthood. Now the mother of two amazing children, one of whom happens to be a brilliant Dyslexic, Lucie has dedicated her time to helping other parents make amazing lives for their kids with Dyslexia.

Douglas C. Curtiss, MD, FAAP

Doug is a pediatrician and a very left-brained thinker. He is also the husband of a Dyslexic and the father of a Dyslexic. Having seen the amazing success of his son in overcoming Dyslexia and using it to create a fantastic life, Doug is amazed at the contrast with some of the children in his pediatric practice who struggle with Dyslexia, not knowing where to turn. As a result, Doug has teamed up with his wife to help all parents and kids with Dyslexia to find the tools and strategies to have a brilliant future.

To Learn More

To learn more about Lucie M. Curtiss and Dr. Douglas Curtiss and watch our videos and leave comments, visit:

www.DyslexicAndUnStoppable.com

Facebook:

Like our page on Facebook.

www.facebook.com/DyslexicUnStoppable

Subscribe to Our YouTube Channel:

www.youtube.com/user/DyslexicUnstoppable

Follow Us on Twitter:

@curtissdc

Please leave feedback on where you bought the book. Thank you!

CPSIA information can be obtained at www.ICGtesting.com
Printed in the USA
BVOW04s0028010916

460749BV00007B/253/P